THIS WASTED LAND

AND ITS CHYMICAL ILLUMINATIONS

by Marc Vincenz
annotated by Tom Bradley
afterword by Siegfried Tolliot

This Wasted Land
and its Chymical Illuminations
by Marc Vincenz
annotated by Tom Bradley.
Copyright © 2014 by Marc Vincenz, Tom Bradley and Lavender Ink
All rites reserved. No part of this work may be reproduced etc.

Printed in the U.S.A.
First Printing
10 9 8 7 6 5 4 3 2   15 16 17 18 19 20

Cover: "Dixie-Fiddle" by Henryk Fantayos © 2014
Book Design: Jonathan Penton and Marc Vincenz

Library of Congress Control Number: 2014960218
Vincenz, Marc.
This Wasted Land and its Chymical Illuminations / Marc Vincenz;
with Tom Bradley (annotator)
p. cm.
Includes Index and Bibliography
ISBN 978-1-935084-72-3 (pbk.)

Lavender Ink
New Orleans
lavenderink.org

Acknowledgments

Earlier abridged versions of excerpts from *This Wasted Land and its Chymical Illuminations* were published in *3 AM Magazine* and *Pirene's Fountain*. Many thanks to their editors.

THIS WASTED LAND
AND ITS CHYMICAL ILLUMINATIONS*

by Marc Vincenz
*annotated by Tom Bradley

Lavender Ink
New Orleans
lavenderink.org
ᴧᴧ

THIS WASTED LAND
AND ITS CHYMICAL ILLUMINATIONS[1]

We had to change the world by rhyme.
–Siegfried Tolliott, *Incantations of a Mad Man*
Edizioni Ermetica, Padua, Italy (limited edition, 1969)

I.   A CERTAIN KIND OF SELF-BURIAL
(THE FRAUDSTER'S DONE)

Most barren yet this damned April[2] land, and the clocks
strike thirteen[3]; pinched within the seething

wild things endure——through faded gauze
of deathly white[4] I dream things that never were,[5]
lilacs[6] hard-wired into the *tick tick tick* of melting ice.[7]   5
                                           Sun-
light deep in reflection, then hardheaded, taunting
this peasant soil in force-fire[8]—still, above,
                                  blue,
blue heaven[9] begins to hum a far less wretched tune   10
of rain and chymical sorcery,[10] coercing tubers and roots

to squirm within sallow layers—and serpents twisting[11]
beyond the line of sight; thawing toads seek beguiling light,[12]
yes, even millipedes tapping into steady locomotion.

                              Through   15
horizon's haze summer swings and swaggers, elbow-
locked with its Southerlies[13]; and your breath upon my ear[14]
in the dimness of that Portobello antique shop, past

busts of Roman flamen, the heavy-handed surveyors
of Babylon, those slave-bearers of Minoan jugs,   20
          the wine

flowing behind the gilded chambers where the spirit
in the hookah unveiled uncertain myths of bipedal bulls,[15]

the lonely tread of empty corridors[16] hidden beneath
         a more substantial world.   25

This, this is the end we start from.[17] And we re-
count inconsequential lives, discover rags of words,

cross off deeds and duties box by box, then eye in eye
and lash and lip seek innocent fluids, visions
        within the inkling   30
           that night
               might become.

      Auch du noch jünger als wie du scheinst, auch wenn
      du so verändert bist. Sei nicht wie du dich selbst siehst.[18]

"As you talk, then so your heart."[19]   35
         And in those early seasons
when stiles and carousels turned,
              when girls tumbled
in grass-stained trousers and little boys voluptuous,
billowing skirts,[20] a simple kiss was all Violet yearned—   40

a peck
on the cheek or the trembling lid, but never the lips
          stained or impaired.

And coffee and wine were grand, as mysterious
as later that obscure emerald tablet,[21] *Kitab sirr al-asrar,*   45

the ocean storm upon her fingers, or that velvet lush
    of Tuscan hills
settling over night's burning vineyards or that Irish
wolf hound moon-talking, cajoling, running circles
beneath the pale turrets of that walled Etruscan city, Lucca.[22]   50

We were not trapped, we were sealed within
        our fates[23]
as wind caressed our skins.
        We caught each other
limb upon extraneous limb[24]   55
        and set ourselves free
in that silence that is full of universal meaning.[25]

Ξ

To Lourdes then, to Lourdes[26] in cherry red,
       water-
speckled among the wedded-hardly-bedded,   60

spinsters and sanctified princesses,[27] missionary bells
and a blessed virgin bearing her luminous child
       to an uninitiated world
       in an irradiant light.

Between the tallest spires shadow wavers   65
        and rock,
rock too is birthed from uncanny loins—as the heart
stammers in words, reaching out through paper-thin
spores—
    as if they might throb deep   70
    in the Earth's fiery core,

vibrating a single cosmic tone[28] and all else should fade
    behind
        everyday's hard liquor.

And yet there was another, a feckless third[29] behind—   75
or far ahead[30] as a fleck upon the iridescent eye.[31]

In walking words belonged to another, perhaps
the woman you were destined to become?[32]

　　Had we, like Narcissus, fallen in love
with the shadows of our own minds?[33]   80

　　Siehst du sie nicht, mein Schatz?
　　Wie sie hinter dir hinkt,
　　nur einen Schritt oder zwei[34]
　　die Katz – in neun Leben vorbei.

"Oh yes, there were flowers too—plucked   85
from a boneyard garden. And on the headstone
chiseled, someone I barely knew
　　　　falling back into lichened stone—
　　　　Mother, a wildflower
that lit up a mountain meadow.   90

　　　　"Or trapped in the amber[35]
that snares stinging gnats, wasps, mosquitoes, fast-
mutating molds scarring innocent hearts."[36]

Missing nothing but words peopled with words[37]—
where the outcome of words is in the council[38]—   95
we drifted to the end of a long, red thread.
　　　　　　You climbed
the fence before me,[39] stumbled, scraped your heavenly knee,
tore the hem of your light summer dress.[40]
　　　　　　　Across fields   100
I bore you, hair pressed limp against dizzying thoughts.

And from the bath's steaming waters you had a vision
of ancestors wielding scimitars and spears, slicing
at barbarous enemies;

      and beyond this Armageddon, dangling   105
from a lone quince in the apple and pear orchard,
a man rotting from his feet to his eyes,

              dead man

singing in a cloud of flies.[41]

Ξ

Hey-ho, hey-ho, all manner of fraudsters and hecklers,   110
readers of palms and psalms who claim archaic knowledge
and offer courteous ethereal introductions
    at the flick
      of a card.[42]

        Siegfried Tolliot,[43]   115
in his caravan, beyond the churchyard with his all-
seeing eyes, an indelible touch—
        fingers that ascertained
the substance of past lives in lockets, pocket watches, earrings,
diamond brooches and plumed heirlooms.[44]   120

"O Diamond! Diamond! You know little
what mischief you have done!"[45]

      Following
purple-haired Cornish coach tourists,
        flimsy shopping bags   125
bearing alms from dusty attics, locked trunks
and secret chambers, we too lined up.

And, at night,
the car park flickered in battery-powered eyes,[46] spied
ancestors crouched behind cars and shrubs, draped   130
over cross spires and clock towers,
      in cloud formations
         and bird formations,
            across passing stars.

      Before these events, many rare birds will cry in the air,   135
      'Now! Now!' and sometime later will vanish[47]

Il ny a un Tarot[48] pour ca. C'est formidable.
C'est plus que grave, Monsieur. The fog bears no shadow.

They have no names in the milky atmosphere, yet they sing
                    like sirens.   140

The mind reels, tied to a mast, the heart burns, roped up.

One cannot be too careful in this age of tragic reason.

$$\Xi$$

Cities, walled cities.[49]
          That judicial right of crenellation.

Walled so high only the chimera might reach   145
the summit, walled to hold the shadows
      in their breach.

Neither here nor there we flowed beneath
baroque eaves and shadowy arches, the darkest,
grimmest tunnels where rodents congregated   150
      in supplication;

and as he foretold, in witness to her madness,
she scored the brick and mortar with raw fingers
leaving her bloody trace throughout the city.

The war's worst was over, but even without   155
      that nightly blaze
of burning showers and that primal scream
                          booming
through walls
      in the silences between chatter,   160
            between cutlery clatter,

those tremors when you gripped the banister,

hands trembled, eyelids twitched, hair thinned.

                  They glared
on Chancery Row beneath their curious   165
bowler brims, along the span of a slowly
      sinking
            London Bridge.

In a hurry to reach a warming hearth
in some dilapidated suburb they sped to wait   170
for a train that was never on time.

            They mumbled

incomprehensibly,[50] mumbled shopping lists
or the Latin names of birds[51] or reptiles or insects.

        "Hatless!"[52]   175

He was quite right. Yes, it was raining again,
just as it had all those weeks on the P & O from Genoa

11

to *Dar es Salaam* when we'd sipped pink gins,
spotted whales,[53]
   cheered bleating porpoises[54]   180
      from rusty rails.

"Ach," so huffed the kiltless Scotsman, drumming up
forgotten words.
      "We walked to Mycenae
and our old boots gave in as water dried up,   185
but still you insisted to plant that single Egyptian seed
in that barren April earth. You know old friend, it grew
into an aging man who writes to me from time to time.[55]

For all his foibles he's become a noted professor of anthropology,[56]
a Socratic fellow[57] with an Aristotelian lump in his throat. 190

       And at night,
staring at the stars, he shakes the sacred spears of Mars.

   Here's his postal address.

You *évolutioniste*, you *logicien*, you fucking *papelard!*"[58]

II.   *What Chess Means to a Hypocrite*

Don't finger the queen.[59]   195

You know there never was
a throne, just a carpenter's chair rocking
along the simplicity of grain,

                     rings of wind
and rain seated on those four stilted   200
                     limbs
turned to creature claws.

               Rocking, she spins
through rough Icelandic wool—
               blankets to fend off nights,   205
bedcovers to shield her from the maddening other.[60]

                    She was no prisoner,
nor a woman kept, more a goddess revered
      from a careful
           distance,   210
             afar.[61]

The king, lacking a pointing finger, had once
been a pacer, now decrepitly slumped

in his own velour, velvet arms thin and frayed,[62]
infernally mumbling, walled in
        over a living grave.[63]
                          And yes,
there were artifacts, trinkets and figurines glaring
from the shelves, in porticos, wall-alcoves, tabletops
and nooks—delving, like that silver-cast winged serpent   220
with the twisted tongue; disarming,
              like that pipa-playing courtesan
with the ivory comb and the wry smile—

reminding him whom he had once squashed
or vanquished,   225
        whom he had loved, if ever he had.

Indeed, candles flickered as eyes blinked
against room-cool evening,
                  weaving
                      in and out   230
of their blue and gold
        and murky zinc
in answer to his own his own his own
wavering breath.

"The source of his life is another   235
and it is but this that causes his breath to flow."[64]

        "Do not become the narrator of your own life!"[65]

Rien, rien, rien ne va plus. From breath to breath
without Temperance to measure the long days,[66]
along frescos of history willfully recorded,[67]   240
        the unknown
footsteps *tick, tick ticked* along corridors, flicked

up and down
the endless—
the stone eternity—   245
the forever stairs.

In such a fashion, long ago he had boarded up
his views to shelter himself from a bleaching light,[68]
that he might feign memory of where the sun rose[69]
and nightly died,   250
     where, at any given breath
     it might now glare down
     in all its heady might
     simply to be
     rather than spite,   255

locked within the branches of which oak or elm
and within,

within the Persian garden
of cypresses and primrose and the strife of love,

or, how, among the green leaves and the tender prickles   260
of the Vermilion Roses, the tincture of a spider's web[70]
sewed the dew together, or—in a dream,

     how the fountains sparkled

in millions of pieces of eight and how the snow-
finches glittered as they watered their wings.   265

Inside,
    frozen,
        moments
        stared him down:
            faces he had scarred,   270

15

men he had feathered and tarred,
women spurned
or seeded.[71]

He knew no children, needed no words
of praise or adoration, for there were no others   275
as empty as he.

The narrator said: "And what are kings,
when regiment is gone, but perfect shadows
in a sunshine day?"[72]

A name plucked from the stars eons ago   280
by another aging soul he daren't call Father:

Sagittarius, planet-watcher, Sagittarius, satyr,
Sagittarius, sidereal, unfingered, stolen king,
shall with goat-feet dance an antic hay.[73]

"Stay away!"   285
        Although I know she wants me in.

"You too will lose your mind, become another kind![74]
A subtle knock will not more likely unlock nor hold
the hounds at bay. Step away and slip back down,
quietly, quietly."

        "Don't you remember the Provence provenance?"[75]   290
        She does. She does. I hear it in her labored breathing.

        "Côtes du Rhône. Trout sautéed in white wine,
        wild boar upon the spit."
        Senses awaken.[76] She moves to the latch.

And the dogs barking night after night. A celebration   295
of a union. Broken voices
egging us on.

The door opens a crack. Dim light flees
down the long corridor.

"There's nothing to celebrate. Nothing at all. Besides   300
I'm afraid meeting a less corrupted
vessel,[77] she'll quietly slither on."

And what of the seed. And the man in Mycenae?[78]

"Oh hold me, fool."
        I do. I do.   305

She's withered having spent
half a lifetime apart from the tree.[79]

"Lost in absentia," she says tenderly, kissing my bristly chin.[80]
I think she means absinthe.
        And the room carousel-spins.   310

Still there is a child within.[81]

And beyond the bed, laid out
in campaign formation: Battle of Waterloo,
Siege at Carnac, Taking of Troy.

Each piece tensely poised,   315
spears at the ready, swords at the draw,
        arrows deployed.

"A white cloud to wipe it all blank. Shadowless."

Hair slips from its bun.
Hair snakes across shoulders.   320
Eyes are dark seeds of dried persimmons.
Breath of autumn, breath of barren earth.
Hands are ice and snow cooling me, covering me
until I feel only white upon white upon hot white.[82]

"Now you are inside. Now you comprehend."[83]   325

  O flee this monstrosity. I urge myself not to gawk.[84]
  Lone women, like to empty houses, perish.[85]

  Yes, there is birth here, but what birth?

  Knees buckle.[86]

  I catch myself among the cobbles,   330
  lunge against walls, prop on battlements,
  surge and stream,
      rippling,
        bubbling,
          seething,   335
            steaming.[87]

If idle chatter will help.[88]

To talk of money—or lack of it. To guzzle and swill
death-defying substances.
To ramble in rolling Umbrian hills   340
where once the sun rose red.

John, yes John is what he says. Or is it James?[89]

It matters not a smidgen, within him he carries a saint.

Either way that hedge fund is dead—
you can't revive it with an offshore address.   345
They'll know. Of course they'll know.

Besides, the Bahamas is run by Americans
who've perfected the art of the tax-dodge, who carry
Switzerland[90] deep in their hearts.

                          In even Congress   350
there is no Trojan horse.
                     And should he be made honest
by an act of government I should not alter
in my faith of him.[91]

Here comes the little woman.[92]   355
How anyone can swagger in stilettos is beyond me.
Baileys on the rocks.
He's on his fifth Canadian Club, neat.
So the money market is dying of
an incurable virus.   360
Guy behind me says:
"Dialectical Materialism,"
as if he's discovered some new-fangled cure.
It doesn't go far.
The saint's woman makes movies.[93]   365
She's buxom buddies with Hollywood rabble-rousers.
Even throws a handful of Scientologists in the mix.
"What's your story?"
Light, polite chat.
Light like the cigarettes I smoke.[94]   370
Light like Diet Coke.
Light like that photon energy that barely
pixelates me—(How I would look
under magnifying glass.) "I'm metro-retro," says the woman.
"*Rosemary's Baby.*[95] Now that was a flick."   375

19

I flick my stub to the floor disgusted
at the lack of ashtrays. Edge my way[96]
to the men's room,
behind the vending machine,
behind the coin-op telephone which now functions   380
as a relic of the future listening into the past.
"Here try these."
                    Red, amber, green.
                                        Go.
Two of each of three.   385

Holy trinity. A prayer for the soul.

One becomes two,
two becomes three,
and out of the third
comes the one as fourth.[97]   390

The lady's room is clean.
Grime still collects in corners.
Roaches doze.
In florescent light, she looks younger—
stretch marks on her breasts are tiger stripes,[98]   395
circles around her eyes make her
a temple-building Egyptian queen
slipping by on a barge on the Nile.[99] O the drums.
And the door locks—from the inside.

HURRY UP PLEASE ITS TIME.   400

Miracle of Velcro,[100] misogyny of clips
between fingertips,
and the zips, the zips, the zips.

The sips, lips, slits.
The whoops, wrangles, the angles.   405

O O O that Freudian slip—[101]
HURRY UP PLEASE ITS TIME.

We're both fools, or so she says
breathing obscenities,
stroking my thighs,   410
pulling my hairs,
electric wires,

and I'm wondering what that hedge fund
actually is, knowing a hedge is a thicket,
a shrub where rabbits breed   415
and wild birds lay speckled eggs.[102]

I wish I'd learned to pick locks,
to cook calves' liver in burgundy.

HURRY UP PLEASE ITS TIME.[103]

And thank God tomorrow it's Sunday.   420
Goodnight John, sorry James.[104] Goodnight Bailey.
Goon-night Canadian Club. Goodnight Diet Coke.
Goodnight folks. Goon-night.[105]

O here comes that envious light.[106]

III.   The Fired-Up-Again Sermon

This is the propensity of getting old,[108] walking   425
the river bank alone as last leaves mold
in gutters, and scaffolding sagging
under planks and tents of tarpaulin.

Eyes scan flowing brown water for signs
of Kraken or *Charybdis*,[109] bobbing of sludge   430

of weed may be the last of the lost
Cretaceous amphibians.[110] But no,

                                    eyes do deceive.

                          As if *La Seine*
or the Yellow River, as if the Ganges   435
with her corpses might denounce Saraswati,
Lakshmi or Parvati;
                  as if Kali[111] and Shiva[112]
and their empty Coke bottles might
sluice away ancient remnants and reawaken   440
as sand creatures, bivalve sifters upon the floor
of an ancient ocean.

22

> Could children swimming
> in city rivers cleanse their souls in city slime?[113]

What has really drifted into the salty ocean?   445
What has really passed in to the liquid song
of the sea?[114] Could it be that Neptune laughs
loudest?
>   Or perhaps the song has departed.

O let it rain, river, let it rain.[115]   450
>   Ahead then,
no magic, no Excalibur to pierce the surface,
no testament of ancient history driving us
to phrases of clairvoyance and clarity.[116]

And behind the shadow slithers,   455
seething in this song muffled by the wind.

Of course there was a rat. There are rats
in every sewer network, in each underground-
underworld, beneath the orderly cities—living off
centuries of detritus across the metrolines   460
of New York, London, Paris, Moscow.
>   Sneaking
through the shantytowns of Rio, of Mumbai,
or in a dingy across Long Island Sound[117]
dodging hypodermics and floating swabs   465
that cleansed cancerous scabs.[118] Rats big as cats,
rats big as lapdogs. *Rattus norvegicus.*

What I might have caught—some mutated from
of river trash—would have snagged
on tooth or nail before I could gut and scale,   470
before I could pepper or sauté.

Perhaps
I should satisfy myself with rat, skinned,
buttered and butterflied flat, pressed pan to pan
roadside, like guinea pigs in the Altiplano   475
flat-griddled crispy golden brown.

O the Incan delights I've come to admire, the brave
souls of experimental food TV, the brave who ingest
beetles, grubs, monkey limbs and fatty dugongs;
                                            who sup
on tripe of any imaginable creature type; and in line   480
with rituals of Neanderthal forbearers, who swear
eating brains will teach you more about your fellow man
than anything in a book—eating brains[119] in the face
of immortality. Words. There's no truth in words.
No truth at all. Talking is the disease of the age.[120]   485

It's all at my back, behind. Unseen, but clinging on.
Memories paced back and forth, a blur; unless
rekindled by a fragrance or a tone. And here she is again.

Dior. Christian Dior. Spice of the Orient.
Femme fatale de la guerre.[121]   490

Amoroso Medium Sweet. And that Lancelot
moving at forty-five degrees,[122] murdering the way
ahead so the empire will survive;
                        Guinevere must survive,
so the walls hold and those battering rams   495
with their wide berth and that parabola Newton's gravity
defined—at least in this king's jaundiced mind.[123]
Traffic surges, stops and purges.
        Lights in their amber,
green and red:[124] a holy trinity. Absurd.   500

24

More noise
than a jungle of carnivores, parrots
                                                        and cavorting monkeys,
a stillness that never arrives and never departs[125]—

dwells even here in my head when the sleepers sleep,   505
when the night rests gently upon the shoulders.

I never did know how to treat women, but they stay
and cradle me into dreams as Mother
                        once did with her rock-a-bye-babies.[126]

Of course, that Southern belle and her Napoleonic   510
old man never withstood my poor mathematical mind.

And her suds, the bath salts, the mare's milk
to keep her skin whiter than china;
                                                        her absinthe,
the fine line of her brittle bones, her chin chiseled[127]   515
to a sculptor's fine point,[128] curtains drawn
upon the last act before poison.

Poison, of course, is in everything,
and no thing is without poison.[129]

Mundane, mundane, mundane day.   520
Whisper of suds on white skin.

pop pop pop pop pop
drip drip drip[130]
toodle pip
tawoo tawitt   525

Walled city.
Stylized, heaven forbid.[131]

Fashion victim among the glitterati.
Walls so high shadows seek each other
within faint spears of light.   530

Yes, I'm a member of the Oxford Club,[132]
paid all my dues and donated enough to build a wing.
But from what I've heard they used my inheritance
for snooker tables handcrafted by the handicapped
in the Black Forest.[133] This is what that scoundrel   535
Hapsburger told me over a draught of bitter and a plate
of bangers and mash just before bombs went off,
before the double-glazed panes shattered.

He was on his way to Calais to strike a match
with four-star Generals, and some-   540
where else—he didn't say[134]—but there was a woman
involved, I'm certain.[135] Yes, the hour was red;
or had been, and yes, I carried on wedging myself
mast and sail in the hope that holding my fingers in front
of my illustrious eyes Captain Cope might not see me.   545
In the hope that others would do all the dogged
chin-wagging. But this was long before we
had conquered all the land, when Earth had a sharp edge;
and so I transformed into one who burned.
I bore my weight, or so they fancied, for gods   550
stole my vision but implanted me with breasts[136]
as Raphael, Botticelli, Messina or Pisanello[137]
might have formed them—with the sharp edge
of vice, with the obtuse angles of their minds.
I daren't speak my name aloud   555
for fear Kali would hear me.[138]
                    Better a woman
than a hound, better a lover than a queen, better
a body of matter than a body of careening
ocean, bitter O better alive than in love again.[139]   560

And why the snakes entwined in lust
                    that I should kill,
should become my own unraveling.[140]
                  Still, Füssli,[141]
not Michelangelo would free me, and unknown words   565
pound in my head, unknown in script or tongue,
return to me again like the fish I've hung
to dry in the Westerlies:[142]

qe-ra-si-ja qe-ra-si-jo qe-ra-si-ja qe-ra-si-jo[143]

The wine we drink is deep red, blood red, love red,   570
revolutionary red, Marxist red as the sky here at dusk.[144]
This is the wine that intoxicated me. And that shriek
that is silent, a breath held to ward off the demons
and rats of my underworld.
                  And here the table   575
we dined upon, the napkins rinsed time and time again,
still hold some faint trace of her lips[145]—that I may kiss
and kiss again. More than kisses, letters mingle souls.
For, thus friends absent speak.[146]

Beyond McDuff,[147]   580
staring out into the distance of television and leather,
and further still, into the distance of internet, upon
these ready-made meals in plastic and cardboard and chalk,
reveal the unwrapped culture I've worshipped—

and there was sand, dark, darker than remembered,   585
sand we slept and cavorted in, sand that molded
to our forms.
        All this rattles inside the mind, even here
at the end of Chinatown as I drown myself in a hot
and spicy soup, in nuggets of Szechuan chicken   590
and peanut, in the flecked patterns of the laminated

tabletops and the mountain ranges beyond Chengdu,
mountain ranges Tamerlane's ancestor's never conquered.[148]
Spirit talk.

qe-ra-si-ja qe-ra-si-jo qe-ra-si-ja qe-ra-si-jo[149]   595

Here she is again. Young. Younger than I remember
when I was young[150]—or is this someone else's nose?[151]
I don't care about the river. I know it can't be her.

Did she really spend all those hours staring into the mirror?[152]
Were her eyes really that wise? Her hair that gold?   600

She said she wanted to fall in love,
yet daren't give in to temptation.
                              Better to be out of love
and wisely alone. Then she bade me farewell, adding:
'Do not forget me!' She vanished, and her departure   605
hurt so much, I woke up…[153]

The king is listening
to the scraping, the shuffling.

Soft shuffle, pitter patter.

Yes, I know. We strolled   610
fingers entwined in Alexandrian knots.[154]
"Divorce me," I said in jest, "untie, or break that knot again."[155]

And buildings seemed foreign
although we had spent months exploring trellised roofs
and one-way lanes, playing architects, playing   615
art historians.
                  Florence and Sienna are such cities,
you can't escape them.[156] Hotels were expensive,

waiters attentive, food explosive, sensations ensnared.
How far away we lived from ourselves.   620

Of course there was the music too.
The ravished soul, being shown such a game,
would break the leashes that tie her to the body.[157]

In the violins and guitar strings, in the stairways
and the verandahs, among the pigeons in the fountains,   625
echoing from wishing wells, in the sycamore trees
and what we felt in Moroccan drums,
figure-eights twisting inside the caverns[158]
of the mind.
              And here, back in New York, downtown,   630
Lower East Side traffic drowns it all out—yet, it throbs too,
through the pavement, through the skin of the soles,
becomes the vibration of the living. To be no part of any body,
is to be nothing.[159] The king is listening

to the scraping, to the shuffling.   635

Soft shuffle, pitter patter.

"The music always seems just beyond me,
yet ever-present."[160] They cling on.
It's as if having once been uttered the phrases
even if unheard, resonate within. Perhaps this is   640
what history is. Illusion,
is the first of all pleasures.[161]

"Surely, this is how jazz becomes
Ionian gold, how Brahms becomes a tree, how a rock
mouths Debussy.   645
          And through the window,
                    off-key,

out into the streets of Basel,
                 a Romanian love song
played on a harmonium, even in the pouring rain,   650
becomes rooftops and walls,
       as drunkards
swoon and stumble
           crooning microbial songs."[162]

The river   655
yearns to sing
as the ocean—
every smear
or blotch,
every loosely-   660
wrought line
or dot,
every letter
or symbol
wants to re-   665
connect with
its primal ink,[163]
wants to re-
vert back
before   670
birth, back
where liquid was
blackened[164]
only by empty space
that was actually   675
not so quite
as empty
as we once thought—[165]
and light was
beginning   680
its journey

yet again.[166]
Hell, to cross
without wind.[167]
Hell without the sail   685
unfurling,
slapping
upon the high bough
and the seagulls
circling,   690
circling,
circling…[168]
You never understood her.
You'll never know
where she goes   695
or what she seeks
where she goes.
Wouldn't we all
want to sing
as the river   700
to the ocean?[169]
Find the wellspring
of the eternally
migrating?

qe-ra-si-ja   qe-ra-si-jo   705
qe-ra-si-ja   qe-ra-si-jo
falalala ladida[170]

"And the blackbirds in winter,
cawing from the rooftops
of the deserted factory
have come from the inner country   710
to eat from the plates of men."

"Yes, yes. We all seek a city to call our body.
Roads, the clogged arteries of the Ur-mother.[171]
License my roving hands, and let them go   715
Before, behind, between, above, below.
O my America! my new-found-land.[172]
But just as New York outgrows me, so Iceland
calls me home, calls me to rest my head
in her lap, in her precious, volcanic soil   720
and hear those missing words of the fire
within the jewel of the mind."
I have measured out my life
in coffee spoons, and hear them calling too.[173]

IV. THUNDER SPEAKS IN FORKED TONGUES

O heaven spent in the mud 725
and more of this autumnal affair,
the animal breathing, careening
the fucking never satisfies, and know
profuse are the kisses of an enemy.[174]
O borderland of the mind 730
where sea and surf meet outcrops,
land where feet tread unsteadily
as if on a ship rolling in the mind.
Profuse the feet on the floor,
the smiles behind the frown. 735
To germinate antique inebriety.
To fashion a child of heart and mind.[175]

V.   *WHAT WATER DROWNS OUT*

After the sweat and the mired grimace, after
plucking the shards of stars from our soles, after
wiping our smiles from cut glass, then—   740
the tired cracks—and in truth, no wonder,

                    as this gestalt beyond
the line of sight now comes alive.

                    And the slow flow
of a barque, oared deep, deep, deep   745
into a watery afterlife.

                    And time, an echo,
            time a cuckoo—

            all gone. *Tada!*
                        KHA.[176]   750
                            Cuckoo.[177]

"O menstrual blood of the sordid whore,[178]
this may just be the language of four-headed dogs!"[179]

34

And those gondalieri, wild ones with their coppery manes,
hardy and thorned.[180] Rare specimens of Nephilim seeded[181]   755
on a sordid beach by Set and his flock of fanatical falcons.
In anticipation of a lifetime of treasures, they clutch
their golden rods, their silver staffs or wave bejeweled spears
to meet a cloven-hoofed father-god—

or some say to kill a giant serpent named Apep.[182]   760

"…and on his shoulder, man, a mercurial ghost;
but those mingling coils of animal souls to light a path
across the water into *this* underworld."

       Imagination then,
       the requisite liquid of fertile soils.   765
       Imagination then,
       how man was created in a deluge.

"Water in the eye, but where's the thunder, Dr. Ripley?"[183]

Is this where the language of four-headed dogs
is the silence upon the valley? *Der Wille zur Macht.*   770

And our kiltless Scotsman,[184] bringing up the rear again,
moving the end of the oar to rest upon his cleft chin:
"Pinch ya nose or the stench'll drag ya low.
This is no Firth of Forth, this is the mother of all.
Hold on. Hold on tight and don't let her go."   775

And I don't, and she doesn't—
until the dissemination of tender graces
and that single index finger displaced, seared
right through the knucklebone. Yet still King Atra-Hasis[185]
points and points ahead,[186] perhaps   780
that is why feel myself

alone within this seething sea of fingers[187]—
unknown even in the annals of the Anunnaki,[188]
but within the lovers all-embracing fire
which burned upon the ziggurat.   785

      O dearest Levant.
      Levant.

One thousand nights and more, justly so
stories, justly right, so, justly so. For fear to know.[189]

Upon the vast horizon, arched in the east,   790
perched high, quoth the crow, quoth the raven,[190] diddling:

Doo-wa-di-di di-di-dum di-di-doo[191]
Fee-fie-fo-fum

As if in baroque jest, as if in the tender harmonies
of a Orleanais gospel choir now washed away.   795
          "O Virginia! How you have grown,
yet how flat you have become!"[192]
           In the crud of my discovery,
a lifetime of singular round
          parallels—   800
            you damn know-it-all,
encircled within a nest
of sorcerers,
     of necromancers,
          of emperors growing   805
            frighteningly cold.[193]

And in the limitless expanse of never-
ending skies, only two towns return
to the triple gem of the mind:

through the Dharma   810
through the Sangha

KHA!

The moon reflected upon the still waters
of Benares, that o-so holy city of the seven,   815
chosen and the most auspicious of all, the Sapta Puri.

KHA.

And—that great other, as espoused by Marco Il Milione
as a city of heaven, the most beautiful in the world,
that great ancient city of Yuhang of the Southern Song   820
where Su Shi, Lu You, and Xin Qiji came to live and die[194]
to expose the sadness of their youth
in rice paper, climbing crooked pagodas,
where *the much* talked incessantly of melancholy,
     then ate the paper sprinkled   825
     in sesame seed washed down
     with sweet plum wine.

And—how too with all that water
returning back to times' end[195] in shantytowns:
São Paulo, Johannesburg and Mumbai,   830
"where the toilet is a road and plastic bags are free-

roaming and
    dreaming,
        dreaming and
            roaming free."—just as Siegfried said,   835

not, Herodotus,[196] that other seer of apparitions,
baker of non-leaven bread, rising so early to beat
the infernal cock-a-doodle-doo of sunlight

meeting uncountable clusters of stubby birds
in the ash of the fallen Hermes tree[197]—   840
just like your own, dear Violet—and you, *you,*
once again, our feckless hooded third, more ablush
than ablaze. Who *is* that really on the other side of you?[198]

I ask: "Is it truly a crime to be in love?"
      "Or perhaps it's better to be concocted?"   845

"Love converts the thing loved into the lover, as the fire,
among all the most active elements, is able to convert
all the other simple and complex elements into itself."[199]

Ξ

November falls into disrepair
as autumn tumbles on wobbly knees—   850
a muted landscape more under the skin
than in the air, and the seagulls twisting and calling:

    "More, More!"[200]

And do you still recall the reek of singed flesh,
that Moorish shashlik,[201] the charcoal on the streets   855
and the bells that kept the hours singing
long into the morning as you lay there
thinking: *Do you know what you have given?*

    O the shame!

Shall we dance? I want to ask, but don't dare—   860
ring around the roses, a pocketful of posies.
I kiss her, I kiss her. *Ma il passione e morte.*
At this the last moment, our third vanishes
into dark flooded corners.[202] You and I forge ahead,

we surveyors of glass words, we invigorators   865
of Malthusian cycles.[203] For soon, for strewth, for sooth,
then strewn upon the battlements,

      line upon line …

KHA

    and   870
        KHA

Cannon-fodder blasting and the alchemist's blue flame
in your night eye as the ancient chant
tolling for who-only-knows,
like a mantra for the inner world, a sky within the skull,   875
Brahmin mahapuranas[204] and the patha of "Om."
Should "I … manifest the works of the Seas:
… the miracles of the deep, shall be exposed."[205]

KHA

Do you hear that crackling of a bestial sun?[206]   880
—then, gone gone, gone beyond, gone altogether beyond,
we reach the shore hand in hand, and like an earnest couple
pronounce ourselves as One. Uno. Einer. Un. Yi ge. Eka.
An apple might be shot from a single head with a crossbow.

"Hark! Is that a leftist battlecry   885
as if left over from the proles?"

And there is little trace of moon-tide,
little left of that once-upon-a-time.
"Sweet Wizard, in whose footsteps I have trod
unto the shrine of the most obscene god,[207]   890
are you the mirror
of my ravished degenerate soul?"

E come quei che con lena affannata, uscito fuor del pelago
a la riva, si volge a l'acqua perigliosa e guata.[208]

           In the middle then.   895

The sundance. Thereafter a trembling fear
of what the thunder might actually say.

Listen: the sound of water
over a rock.

Khanti![209] O blessed one.   900
      Khanti.
           Cuckoo.

AFTERWORD
by Siegfried Tolliot

Thow hast written me, but yet dost not know me.

—John Dee, *De Heptarchia Mystica (Diuinis, Ipsius Creationis, Stabilis Legibus)*

The primary text of this volume speaks for itself, like all true poetry (Eliot's annotation of *The Waste Land* notwithstanding). I'm no more qualified to re-orchestrate the *Jupiter Symphony* than to do anything but stand back and be stunned by Marc Vincenz's work. That is why, when the editors asked me to write this afterword, I was puzzled[*]—until I noticed hundreds of tiny numbers popping up between the words, impeding the elemental flow of the Vincenzian strophe no more effectively than gravel diverts an Alpine stream in springtime spate.

---

[*] The present annotator is still puzzled.

41

"The present annotator" (as he insists on calling "him/herself") would be recognizable even if Tom Bradley's name did not appear underneath Marc Vincenz's on this book's cover. *His near-superhuman erudition and virtuosic grasp of English prose are widely acknowledged, along with the effortless, playful, and, yes, beautiful way he can toss around blocks of rhetoric and arcana that would crush other writers.*[†] But proportional shortcomings always attend extraordinary native gifts; and, in Tom Bradley's case, the foibles can only be categorized as moral.

His relentless libel of one of Vincenz's fellow poets is too heavy-handed to bother refuting. The reader can draw his/her own conclusions as to the plausibility of the shenanigans that unfold among these annotations, in a narrative fragmented as yesteryear's most self-conscious metafiction.[‡] Nothing more needs to be be said on the topic, except this: Bradley's sociopathy extends beyond the unscholarly to the interpersonal. Hence his ability to seduce indiscretions via private

---

[†] Emphasis added by the present annotator.

[‡] The present annotator fails to see how the live, on-air incapacitation of a major television network's anchorwoman (see note 43), the molestation of a distinguished modernist in a mental institution (see note 80), and the misappropriation of student tuition fees to bankroll extended "pilgrimages" to the strange cult centers of Coeur d'Alene, Idaho (see note 167), can be dismissed as mere "shenanigans."

email correspondence.§ Professional envy is indicated, and socioeconomic class resentment: the victim of his fabrications happens to be Professor Emeritus of Creative Writing at a fully accredited institution of tertiary education.¶

Bradley's sour academic grapes betray his own well-known chronic unemployment and multiple decade-long damnation to wandering exile among the TEFL trash of the extreme Orient—which, oddly, he seems to consider a point of pride. Witness the potted bio that appears in conjunction with every appearance of his name, in print or pixel:

> *Doctor* [sic] *Bradley fucked permanently off from America in 1985, moved to Red China, and has lurked around the left rim of the Pacific ever since, in a successful search for sinecures that steal virtually no time and absolutely no mental energy from his writing.*

---

§ Those indiscreet email messages were forced on the present annotator, sent and re-sent enough times to trigger the spam filter—unsurprising behavior in a notorious literary stalker.

¶ Panguitch Community College's accreditation has been up for review several dozen times in nearly as many years.

If the five volumes of his *Sam Edwine Pentateuch* are to be accepted as autobiography, this "successful search for sinecures" has been undertaken on the strength of a fake Ph.D. diploma ordered from the back pages of *Hustler Magazine*. No record exists of this particular "Tom Bradley" having attended so much as a baccalaureate program, much less undergoing the rigors that would have earned him the coveted Master of Fine Arts degree. He has failed to qualify himself to join our profession as mentor to America's burgeoning crop of young poets in their glorious hundreds of thousands: a flowering of literature unprecedented in recorded history; a community of writers that, by sheer numbers alone, shames Periclean Athens, Augustan Rome, Elizabethan London and Impellitterian New York City.

With a perfunctory glance at the critical apparatus feeding like a parasite off *This Wasted Land,* it's easy to see how an academic career has eluded Bradley. In an obvious attempt to ram a middle finger into scholarship's eyeball, again and again he flouts the Modern Language Association's Style Sheet. He employs an interrogative pronoun long ago expunged from English by that august body. He neglects to observe the most basic bibliographical rule: *thou shalt name the author of the book thou citeth*—who happens, in several cases, to be Bradley himself. Compounding self-promotion with insufferable coyness, he anonymously refers to his own impressive list of titles (nearly thirty ISBNs now in print).[**]

Do the editors of this book expect me to disclaim Bradley's mental instability, apologize for his unbalanced political obsessions, hoot at his fatuousness (demonstrated by his doctrinaire Blavatskianity), and decry his *referential mania*—to use a term coined by Vladimir Nabokov, his pedophiliac ideal?

I suspect such peccadillos are not all that have kept him out from behind the professorial podium. Displaying what can only be described as flippant disregard for intellectual rigor, Bradley has sunk alongside T. S. Eliot into "remarkable expositions of bogus scholarship." He indulges in deliberate non-sequitur, which he no doubt dignifies as "impressionistic analysis." For example:

> *Jennifer Jones, who starred eponymously in* Song of Bernadette, *was born on the day of the eldest Fatima seer's death. That year Boston got flooded with molasses, in the sort of synchronicity whose pertinence the occult mind apprehends instantaneously as the remembrance of a Proustian madeleine....*

[**] See tombradley.org

This "synchronicity" degenerates into the all-too-familiar pseudo-Buddhistic expedients found useful by annotators intent on padding out their research with licentious free-association: removing tense from time, treating gender like taffy, rendering prepositions interchangeable:

> *... The foregoing itinerary, if it bears no relation to carto-*
> *graphic reality, serves to reassert the flexibility of spatial-*
> *ity....*

Surprisingly, for all his polymathic reputation, at one point Bradley displays ignorance of the most familiar line in modernist poetry, as cited by Mr. Vincenz toward the end of his penultimate canto: *I have measured out my life with coffee spoons.* "The present annotator" appends the following note:

> *In Appalachian jug bands, the favorite percussion instru-*
> *ments for marking time, or "measuring out the life" of*
> *a tune, are the doubled spoons, clattered against dunga-*
> *reed thighs or washboarded across menial labor-callused*
> *fingers. If these uncouth utensils can't be said to produce*

the Root Tone of Nature, they do doubly thunder like the
forked tongue that announces our next canto.

But I assume I was not asked to write this afterword to drive positively every reader away. So, what can be said in Bradley's favor? Well, for one thing, his religio-political spleen, while bordering on paranoid schizophrenia, is interfaith: cf. his incessant harping on "pedophile priestcraft." (Of course, it's not his anticlericalism that will get him into trouble.)

I can say that Bradley's notes come close to being redeemed by his unfeigned (and unrequited) esteem for "our poet." It's an admiration unbased on systematic analysis of Vincenz's formidable opus, yet all the more moving for that: a visceral reaction rare in contemporary criticism. It is with relish that Bradley *eats from the plate* of this most *sublimely culinary of living poets.* This must exacerbate the pain and humiliation Bradley surely feels when, toward the end of the poem, finally fed up with all the mad muttering underfoot, Vincenz sends down a rebuke: *you damn know-it-all.* A few lines later, he even consigns Bradley to death by *drowning in dark corners.*[††] Endnote 193 is

---

†† At least our poet doesn't dismiss the present annotator's verse as a "seething sea of fingers." (See note 187 for Pound's critical appraisal of Tolliot's *throbbing dactyls.*)

a desperate attempt to write this off as a mere moment of crankiness brought on by fatigue.

He does show a modicum of insight into his own murky self with his citation of two other literary men whose sarcasm got them, too, banished from their homelands. How does this lifelong expatriate evoke unemployable Giordano Bruno and unsocializable Juvenal? By an anonymous reference to one of his own books, of course. See Bradley's 199th endnote for an admittedly affecting comparison of Juvenal's grim exilic outpost to the extreme Orient, "where I languish now."

For all his emotional deformity, psychosexual infantilism and shortage of diplomas, Bradley's simultaneously shrewd and profound reappraisal of *The Cantos* is among the few justifications for the existence of this otherwise at-best nugatory contribution to the magnificent Vincenzian *oeuvre*. The editors were on the verge of blue-penciling the entire substructure, but for Bradley's original research and solid contribution to the lively field of Poundian biographical studies, productive of so many Ph.D. dissertations with every new academic year, including the efforts of more than a few of my teaching assistants, who I chaperone on pilgrimages north to Hailey, Idaho each winter—

though we'd have to take a circuitous route indeed, if, as Bradley asserts, we stopped off at Coeur d' Alene "on the way back."‡‡

—Panguitch, Nevada, 2013

---

‡‡ See note 167 for Tolliot's willing lionization by neo-Nazi intelligentsia and barter economists in that far-northern Idaho burg.

NOTES

1. The prototypical instance of such illumination took Christian Rosenkreutz in ambush, as it were, in his *Chymical Wedding*:

   > *...somebody in an unusual manner touched me on the back; whereupon I was so hugely terrified, that I durst hardly look about me....I looked back, and behold it was a fair and glorious lady....*

   Our subtitle is a veiled prompt to the reader to expect enlightenment from behind. Since a book, when being engaged, is always positioned in front of the face, the rear that is being brought up so luminously must be situated in *tenseful time*. (Cf. note 18, Einstein's "stubborn illusion.")

   According to the formulation of the maker of *Pale Fire*, that other annotated poem—

   > *...one cannot read a book: one can only re-read it. A good reader, a major reader, an active and creative reader is a re-reader.*
   > —*Lectures on Literature*

Since scholarly usage as well as popular idiom places read lines "above," illumination, like ultraviolet rays from *blue heaven* (see line 9), must shine on the *re-reader* from that quarter (difficult as it is to admit for a composer of end notes). For light to come from both behind and above, the percipient must be prostrate, as with reverent and prayerful awe. Thus our subtitle apprises the *re-reader* of the correct posture to assume, and the appropriate attitude to take, toward our poem, along with any critical apparatus that might subtend.

2. On the Kalends of *Aprilis*, Rome celebrated the *Veneralia* in honor of their heavenly mother, Venus Heart-Changer, to whom they consecrated a temple in expiation of the crime of orgiastic incest committed by two of her vestal virgins, Aemilia and Licinia. (Cassius Dio, *Roman History*, Liber XXVI)

Already, before the end of the first line, a pair of sexual malefactors is confronting us head-on (*i.e.*, burrowing up from beneath our bellies, as we are in missionary position). *Barren* and *damned*, inspiring anything but reverent and prayerful awe, by the very proverbiality of their names they contradict the *fairness* and *gloriousness* of the *lady* who tapped our shoulder in the Rosicrucian subtitle. Not only is enlightenment to be expected from behind, but the *ignis fatuus*. (See note 11.)

Compare Adam's rebuke to a much more formidable female than these naughty vestals:

> *I will not lie beneath you, but only on top.*
> *For you are fit only to be in the bottom position,*
> *while I am to be the superior one.*
> *—Alphabet of Sirach*

(For Lilith, see note 120.)

3. *It was a bright cold day in April, and the clocks were striking thirteen.*
   —Orwell, *1984*

4. *pinched...deathly white*

In Gaza under the Roman Empire, Chinese fabrics delivered from
the Silk Road were picked apart (*pinched within seething* fingertips)
and rewoven into translucent *gauze*, named after the city. These
sheer tissues were stained the lubricious hue of the *lilacs* that begin
our fifth line, with a dye distilled from the soft parts of meat-eating
sea snails who make their home off Tyre, further up the Mediterranean coast. Translucent garments were confected from this gauze,
for delivery to the capital, to swathe and render more alluring the
nakedness of pathics on the Palatine, and to accentuate the unchas-
tity of Aemilia and Licinia's moral descendants.

But here the gauze is yet undyed—therefore unexported. Still stuck
in Gaza, the *wild things* must *endure*, rather than go frolic in Rome.
This recalls two *deathly whitenings* in the same Palestinian municipality, at the end of the Period of the Judges (ca. 1050 B.C), and
during the so-called "War" of 2008-9 :

> *White phosphorize my orbits both*
>   *and damn me straight to Gaza.*
> *Slam me in the dark like eyeless*
>   *Samson on his pillar,*
> *chained by Philistines and mocked*
>   *by theriomorphic gods.*
> *I tend to write my best when facing*
>   *worse than even odds.*
> —*We'll See Who Seduces Whom*, Canto VIII (Unlikely
> Books, 2013)

Here we have a more lethal transgression than mere sexual license—though the intimate deoxyribonucleic relation of oppressor to victim does carry hints of the *crimen incesti,* as follows:

> [The Ishmaelite sons of Hagar and the seed of Abraham in the line of Isaac] *share a common pool of Y-chromosome biallelic haplotypes....*
> —Hammer MF, Redd AJ, Wood ET, et al., in the *Proceedings of the National Academy of Sciences of the United States of America 97,* June 2000.

It will be seen in *This Wasted Land* that such diaphanous articles of *gauze* are not always donned to carnal purpose. Occasionally one of our own *Venus Heart-Changers* will beautify herself with suggestive textiles to enhance the percipient's spiritual ecstasy. (See lines 604-6 and note 153.)

Mina Loy knew this well:

> *Virgins may whisper*
> *"Transparent nightdresses made all of lace"*
> *Virgins may squeak*
> *"My dear I should faint"*
> *Flutter ... ...flutter ....flutter...*
> —from *Virgins Plus Curtains*

(Cf. note 187 for Ezra Pound's ecstatic reaction to this *fair and glorious lady*'s literary manifestation.)

5. The more recent of the two "deathly whitenings" mentioned above was made possible, if not inevitable, by another "War," even briefer than the one in 2008–9, which was waged forty-one years earlier in the same place of *gauze.* Robert F. Kennedy's support for a particular side of that war got him assassinated exactly one year after the

second of its six days. He is popularly assumed to have originated the following apothegm:

> *You see things; and you say, "Why?" But I dream things*
> *that never were; and I say, "Why not?"*

But, of course, it hisses from between the hollow fangs of the Serpent in *Back to Methuselah*, by George Bernard *"The Nazi movement…has my warmest sympathy"* Shaw.

In the more philosemitic realm of American politics, a corrupted version of these two sentences was first uttered by the older brother of Sirhan Sirhan's victim. (See note 52 for the scandalous plane ride back from Dallas.) Teddy Kennedy, in his turn, when the time came, took it upon himself to garble the Shavian original even further, continuing one of the most widely spread hashes of misattribution of recent times. The matter is alluded to here, already in our fourth line, to prepare us for a plunge into the mélange of multiple mimicry, false physiognomy and gleeful literary piracy that is *This Wasted Land.*

6. *Lilac and star and bird twined with the chant of my soul,*
    There in the fragrant pines and the cedars dusk and dim.
    —Walt Whitman

The *pines* are of Hebron, and the *cedars* are of Lebanon.

7. The melting ice drips like *white-phosphorized* flesh off Ishmaelite bones (cf. note 4), or aqueous humor from Samson's eye sockets—or, indeed, like another bodily liquid to which the murderous element owes its discovery, in 1669, in the alchemical laboratory of Hennig Brandt The latter described the inefficient process to his friend Leibniz as follows:

Boil urine to reduce it to a thick syrup. Heat until a red oil distills up from it, and draw that off. Allow the remainder to cool, where it consists of a black spongy upper part and a salty lower part. Discard the salt and mix the red oil back into the black material. Heat that mixture strongly for sixteen hours. First white fumes come off, then an oil, then phosphorus. The phosphorus may be passed into cold water to solidify.

Western alchemists, no less than Rosicrucians, drew much illumination from the *fair and glorious lady* in her various guises. They symbolized their sixth operation, Distillation, with the constellation Virgo, depicted by John of Patmos as a woman disguised in sunlight, *i.e.,* Queen of Heaven, Mary the Mother of Christ:

And there appeared a great wonder in heaven; a woman clothed with the sun, and the moon under her feet, and upon her head a crown of twelve stars.
—Revelation 12:1

In the *urtext* from which T. S. Eliot improvised the fragmentary bits of his March Hare inventions (see notes 17 and 27), this queen is clothed not in the sun, but in a party dress. She seems to be given credit for the discovery of white phosphorous. The "jolly tinker" is the alchemist Hennig Brandt himself (recast in Eliot's fragments as self-portraiture: cf. notes 10 and 17).

My Lady she was dressing
Dressing for the ball
When she saw the jolly tinker
Lashing piss *against the wall* [emphasis added]

In Hennig Brandt's down-to-earth case, Mary was rather Margaret, who made herself manifest not as mother, but wife. The light she brought was chemical rather than celestial, and her inspiration consisted not of inner locutions, but a large material dowry. This permitted her husband to concentrate on his search for the universal elixir, which entailed the Herculean labor of accumulating and storing more than 5,000 liters of *piss*.

That such work can be bent indifferently to good or evil purpose, by sage or sorcerer, is well understood by the Chinese. In Mandarin, *Wu* is used in compounds like *wugu* 巫蠱 "sorcery; the casting of harmful spells," *wushen* 巫神 or *shenwu* 神巫 (with *shen* "spirit; god"), "wizard; sorcerer," and *wuxian* 巫仙 (with *xian* "immortal; alchemist"), "immortal shaman."

Thanks to the supremely practical Phoenicians and their bills of lading, the present annotator is in a position to be obliged to Marc Vincenz for pictographical arcana such as the foregoing. See note 52 for a poem by a major modernist with no firmer grasp on the Middle Kingdom's hieroglyphs than Francesco Colonna had on Egypt's. (Cf. line 261 for the latter's *Hypnerotomachia Poliphili*.)

8. In Frazer, "the flickering light of the Golden Bough" is ignited in neither alembic nor cucurbit, but rather in the hovel, by a process more folksily magical—simple friction—and employed as a cure for the plague. See note 129 for combusting wood as an object lesson in alchemy's *tria prima*, and note 36 for Thales' frottage with materials other than twigs and sticks.

9. *Where a wind ever soft from the blue heaven blows...*
   —Lord Byron, *The Bride of Abydos* (1813)

10. *taunting this peasant soil…sorcery*

Most of the unfortunates upon whom *sorcerous rain* is *pissing* from *blue heaven* originally sprang from the *peasant soil,* but were *taunted* and *forced* by *fire* to proletarianize in this long-troubled town.

> *The Astral Light has been taken too literally to mean some sort of a second* blue sky. *This imaginary space, however, on which are impressed the countless images of all that ever was, is, and will be, is but a too sad reality. It becomes in, and for, man…a tempting Demon, his "evil angel," and the inspirer of all our worst deeds.*
> —The Transactions of the Blavatsky Lodge, 1889

So far, as of line 11, the worst deeds in *This Wasted Land* have been inspired by the jolly tinkering of Hennig Brandt *qua* T. S. Eliot, our *evil angel* and *tempting Demon.* As the latter famously reminds us, the weaponization of white phosphorus is not unknown in Christendom (cf. note 89: *a friendly spout of liquid fire*).

Cf. note 120: Isaiah's precognition of YHWH's deployment of chemical weapons, which his Iron Age imagination saw as combusting pitch and brimstone.

11. *tubers…twisting*

> *The Circus or Hippodrome was a stately building about four hundred paces in length and one hundred in breadth. The space between the two metae or goals was filled with statues and obelisks; and we may still remark a very singular fragment of antiquity, the bodies of three serpents twisted into one pillar of brass. Their triple heads had once*

supported the golden tripod which, after the defeat of Xer-
xes, was consecrated in the temple of Apollo at Delphi, by
the victorious Greeks.
—Gibbon, *The Decline and Fall of the Roman Empire*

Cf. note 105 for a helix with one less reptile.

This is the work of Madame Blavatsky's "Ophiomorphos, ser-
pent-shaped spirit of all that is basest in matter," the shoddy product of demiurgic Ialdabaoth, the *ignis fatuus* (see note 2). With the
recruiting assistance of *sorcery*, this *evil angel* of the Sun (Astral)
Light (cf. note 10) *coerces* the *twisting* of *serpents* and *squirming* of
roots.

The *tubers* and *roots* in question are the emergent bones of the
alchemically pissed-upon. The *sallow layers* they squirm within are
Ishmaelite epidermis, jaundiced by poverty and daily urolagnic
humiliation at the hands and clipped phalli of border guards. Skel-
etomusculature is *coerced* to *twist* and *squirm* as skin melts away
under the white phosphoric downpour.

Coercion is not too strong a term, as the Jewish mystics knew:

Against your will you become an embryo, and against your
will you are born.
—*Mishnah Aboth* IV.29

12.   *Light, seeking light, doth light beguile.*
       —Shakespeare, *Love's Labour Lost*

13. *elbow...southerlies*

Our poet stands in *This Wasted* ["Promised"] *Land*, shoulder-to-shoulder with the beleaguered Ishmaelites, facing squarely the [al-]chemical weaponry deployed from the East (further into Asia, where neither Reformation, Renaissance nor Enlightenment ever took place). Suddenly he feels in his right ear the whispering Southerly wind. It's his *fair and glorious lady*, his Queen of Heaven, his alchemical initiatrix. She penetrates him via the auditory meatus, like the Holy Spirit fecundating the Blessed Virgin with the Word to be made flesh, as follows:

> *Come and gaze upon this marvellous feat: the woman conceives through the hearing of her ears!*
> —Athanasius of Alexandria

> *Like the Burning Bush on Horeb which carried God in the heart of the flames, so Mary brought Christ into her virginity: through her ear the Divine Word of the Father entered and dwelt secretly in her womb.*
> —Ephrem of Syria

Our poet's insufflator is to be identified with Sophia, in many Gnostic traditions the Third Person of the Trinity and syzygy of Christ (cf. *shakti*, notes 111 and 171). This is but one among numerous instances in our poem of gender reversal, if not transsexualization outright. (See below, passim.)

Strange to say, the Valentinians considered the Demiurge, Ialdabaoth (see note 11), to be a monster spawned by Sophia. Are we to view *This Wasted Land*, the child of of our poet's inseminated cranium, in that false light? The original transaction upon which this system of imagery is based wasn't always seen through rosy lenses:

> *That Christ was a bastard and his mother dishonest... That the angel Gabriel was bawd to the Holy Ghost, because he brought the salutation to Mary.*
> —Richard Baines' note to Queen Elizabeth's privy council, containing several accusations of "blasphemy" on Christopher Marlowe's part.

(See notes 91, 94, 104 and 192.)

We have been warned from the outset that the *ignis fatuus* might come from above and behind. So visitation from the side, particularly dextrous, carries a greater guarantee of validity than any mere Romish *nihil obstat*. Note how in her approach our poet's wind-blown Wisdom distinguishes herself from the demoness Lilith, who Adam attempted to consign to the submissive coital position. (See note 2; but cf. note 164, where Terence McKenna's loathsome *nigredo* hag also assumes a lateral motion, presumably sinister.)

Perhaps a form of quasi-Jungian *contrasexualization* is engaged here (cf. note 99), and our Sophia has a scrotum flapping in the breeze, after all. An Italian word for the *southerly* wind is *ostro*. This pair of rounded-vowel syllables enlist the *coercive sorcery* of neither Logos nor Demiurge (cf. note 17), but a *man*—though his mortality has been questioned since the late summer of 1795.

At the end of the Mediterranean opposite from *ostro*-blown Italy, sixty kilometers inland from the shore where the carnivorous Murex gastropods were gathered and drained of their lubricious *lilac* color (see line 5), the Jews' City of God stands on its contested hill. In the language of the Phoenicians (close cousins: see note 4), this category of municipality was called a *karel*. From that word are derived the other two syllables of *Cagliostro*'s name.

We have *locked elbows* with the greatest European sorcerer of post-antiquity, and an alchemist of upper-middling accomplishment. Once again the gonadal tables have been turned. In one of his many female guises, Cagliostro is engaging us by means of an invisible motion of air, the very sort of inner locution by which such adepts effect their posthypnotic suggestions, and hermaphrodite apparitions exhale gnosis into poets' ears.

Included among Cagliostro's self-proclaimed feminine excarnations is Aleister Crowley, with his penchant for submissive sodomy and his musculature "like a Victorian maiden." (*Autohagiography*). Cf. note 207 for an instance where Crowley turned the gonadal tables on himself, at least figuratively, and, for once in his magickal career, *pitched* rather than *caught*, with the assistance of Victor Benjamin Neuburg. (See lines 889-90, for a heroic couplet written by that sorcerer's sore apprentice.)

Meanwhile, back at the kibbutz, the singer of the *Song of Songs* stirs the same *southerly* and finds it stimulative of profitable produce:

> *Awake, O north wind; and come, thou south; blow upon my garden, that the spices thereof may flow out. Let my beloved come into his garden, and eat his pleasant fruits.*
> —4:16

Later, in his sad dotage (presumably the seventy-two demons in his famous jar had failed to fulfill his desires beyond a bumper crop of emerald-green grapefruits: see note 163), Solomon took this same sublime meteorological phenomenon and bent it to nihilistic purpose. The "preacher" that the wise king became with senescence bewailed the kosher *ostro* as a treadmill of vexatious vanity:

> *The wind goeth toward the south, and turneth about unto the north; it whirleth about continually, and the wind returneth again according to his circuits.*
> —Ecclesiastes 1:6

As is often the case, incessant cycles of contradiction suggest that our poet is being prepared for initiation into a mystery:

> *Those who are to be baptised are insufflated by the priest of God, so that the Prince of Sinners may be put to flight*

from out of them, and that entry for the Lord Christ might
be prepared, and that by his insufflation they might be
made worthy to receive the Holy Spirit.
—Magnus of Sens, *Libellus de mysterio baptismatis*

On the verge of being puffed like a hookah by the gnostic lips of
Sophia, our poet is reminded, by this wind, of the beauty that's
coming his way, and its inevitable dying down at the end of the
last verse on his long poem's final page. But, as we have been
schooled in *re-reading*, the poetry will continue to circulate like
planetary atmosphere.

Such cyclical motion implies a subcontinental wisdom only available to the exoteric Western mind on the unconscious level. Our
poet, with the help of his annotator (faithful, if occasionally un-
derappreciated: cf. lines 801 and 862-3), makes all explicit.

14. *your breath upon my ear*

Here, for the first time, our poet apostrophizes his *fair and glorious*
lady who is supernaturally making her whispered revelation heard
over the screaming Apache helicopters. By engaging her with direct speech (cf. note 170 for *invocation*), Vincenz courageously
enlists himself among our poem's numerous *dramatis personae* of
seers, alchemists, prophets and charlatans, all similarly schooled
and/or ridden by testicularly unenumbered spirits. (See below,
passim.)

15. *busts of Roman flamen…bipedal bulls*

Sublimity having sidled through the thick of the grossest politicide, our poet is translated from this strip of Gehenna to a balmy

dream of antiquity. He and his Sophia waft on conjoined syzygic wings to Italy, Lower Mesopotamia, Crete, even the quicksands off the northern African coast—

> *...And steers toward the Syrtes where the southerlies hold sway,*
> *or sails the seas he knows not where.*
> —Horace, Epode IX

—anywhere but the lurid Levant. The rubble of Herod's formerly splendiferous town hall attracts no more notice in our first canto than its precursor received from Herodotus.

16. *Down thought's long echoing corridors, though behind*
     Some lingering sense of it may still remain.
     Such is the past of lovers: dear delight,
     Sweet lips that kissed sweet eyes that wept for me...
     —Evelyn Douglas, *"As the faint ghost of a forgotten strain"*

17. The twenty-sixth line of this poem for *re-readers* comprises an exhortation to look back to the first: an Eliotian rendering in tenseful time of our behind-and-above paradox. (Cf. note 1.)

> *In my beginning is my end...*
> *In my end is my beginning...*
> —"East Coker"

> *What we call the beginning is often the end*
> *And to make an end is to make a beginning.*
> —"Little Gidding"

In these passages, Eliot, our own poem's *tempting Demon* and *Evil Angel* (see note 10), in agreement with numerous critics and poets, proclaims his *oeuvre* to encompass twentieth-century poetry. In this he recapitulates the hubristic Christ of Saint John's Apocalypse:

> *I am Alpha and Omega, the beginning and the end, the first and the last.*
> —Revelation 22:13

Christians find their founder not only explicit in the last verse of Revelation but implicit in the first verse of Genesis, as follows:

> *In the beginning God created the heaven and the earth.*

John's Gospel restates it in Greek terms:

> *In the beginning was the Word, and the Word was with God, and the Word was God.*

Christ is therefore identified with the Logos, and as such does the work of creation, the chore of Ialdabaoth:

> *This Demiurgic errand boy, this mope,*
> *gets gussied up as pretty as a pope.*
> *To take this bungling spastic fucker-up*
> *of our particular niggling solar clump,*
> *and puff him into That Unthinkable,*
> *unreachable by either praise or blame,*
> *entails the sickest blasphemy of all.*
> —*We'll See Who Seduces Whom,* Exode (2013)

This creator-creature who cooks up (and fucks up) existence through the heat of the Sun (Astral) Light appears as a self-portrait among Eliot's suppressed fragments, as follows:

> *There was a jolly tinker came across the sea*
> *With his four and twenty inches hanging to his knee.*

With his long-pronged hongpronged
Underhanded babyfetcher
Hanging to his knee.

It was a sunny summer day the tinker was in heat
With his eight and forty inches hanging to his feet...

With his whanger in his hand he walked through the hall
"By God" said the cook "he's come to fuck us all."
—*Inventions of the March Hare: Poems 1909-1917*

Note how the generative organ of Eliot's alter ego grows double along its vertical axis, the better to *penetrate every solid thing* (cf. note 21). This is an occult process long acknowledged by gnostics as well as kabalists, Jew and gentile alike:

The binary is the fundamental corner-stone of Gnosis. As the binary is the Unity multiplying itself and self-creating, the kabalists show the "Unknown" passive En-Soph, as emanating from himself, Sephira, which, becoming visible light, is said to produce Adam Kadmon.
—Helena Petrovna Blavatsky, *Isis Unveiled*, Vol. 2, Chapter VI

Philo Judaeus identifies Adam Kadmon with the Logos. Thus, Eliot, the *poet* (from Greek *poetes*, "maker"), increasing his *long-pronged hongpronged / Underhanded babyfetcher* by a factor of two, is applying for the job of the Trinity's second person. Hence his subsequent craven conversion to Anglicanism (entailing in part a pornographic recasting of Mariolatry: see note 27), and his adolescent blaspheming of Madame Blavatsky, whose anti-Christian polemics make Nietzsche look like the Lutheran pastor's boy he is. Our *tempting demon* and *evil angel* has yet fully to earn such a formidable pair of sobriquets.

18. Another exhortation to the *re-reader* to exercise hindsight, and to question the ostensible illumination of tenseful time, which, in personal correspondence, Albert Einstein, that great fan of Madame Blavatsky (a.k.a. the Mighty and Ineffable Pythoness of Dnepropetrovsk), described as a "stubbornly persistent illusion." This is millennia-old news in Theosophical circles.

19. This is a maxim from the laboratory of Philippus Theophrastus Aureolus Bombastus von Hohenheim, introducer of Rome's divine blacksmith into alchemy's pantheon, as follows:

    Nothing has been created as ultima materia—in its final state. Everything is at first created in its prima materia, its original stuff; whereupon Vulcan comes, and by the art of alchemy develops it into its final substance.

    Creation's chore has been further delegated to a metal-working manifestation of Eliot's *tinker in heat*. Like Cagliostro, Vulcan is more third-hand artisan than second-hand demiurge. Locked in the elbow of the former, manacled with the adamantine chains of the latter, we are are being frog-marched ever downward, step-by-step closer to the mortal sort of maker who forges verse rather than planets, whose *talk* is not of Logos, but rather more of the preexisting *heart*.

    Our poet is making his entrance as Poet, *whanger in his hand,* all the more glorious for human bathos.

20. The strange transvestite children have their astral reflection in the vast variety of ambiguously sexed manifestations to be encountered throughout these pages, e.g., the previous canto's insufflator (both virgin and impregnator). Matter-mired counterparts include a

vaginoplasticized Commander of the Most Excellent Order of the British Empire (line 551), a *priapic eunuch* who romps and lurks passim, the present annotator him/herself, and the proverbial Tiresias, *uniter of all the rest* (cf. note 32)—though the latter, unique to this catalogue, underwent a reversible gender reassignment.

21.   *that obscure emerald tablet*

This is Hermes Trismegistos' *Tabula Smaragdina*—not as lifted by the mother of the Jews from the corpse in the Hebron cave, but rather the edition which Apollonius of Tyana, during his sojourn in the Egyptian port city, pried from the cadaverous fingers of Alexander the Once-Great, who earlier, marvelous to relate, personally pried it from those of Thrice-Great Hermes.

Newton's Englishing of this Emerald Tablet, discovered posthumously among the few alchemical papers left unburnt by his dog (see line 121), is as follows:

Tis true without lying, certain & most true.

That which is below is like that which is above & that which is above is like that which is below to do the miracles of one only thing. (Cf. line 716 for John Donne on the flexibility of prepositions of space, and note 30 for Saint Peter's dying words to similar effect.)

And as all things have been & arose from one by the mediation of one: so all things have their birth from this one thing by adaptation.

The Sun is its father, the moon its mother, the wind hath carried it in its belly, the earth is its nurse. (Cf. note 99 on lunar *leucosis* and solar *xanthosis.*)

The father of all perfection in the whole world is here.

Its force or power is entire if it be converted into earth.
(Thales considered that water undergoes such a conversion: cf. note 36.)

Separate thou the earth from the fire, the subtile from the gross sweetly with great industry.

It ascends from the earth to the heaven & again it descends to the earth & receives the force of things superior & inferior.

By this means you shall have the glory of the whole world & thereby all obscurity shall fly from you.

Its force is above all force. For it vanquishes every subtile thing and penetrates every solid thing [emphasis added]. Cf. note 17: "…he's come to fuck us all."

So was the world created.

From this are & do come admirable adaptations whereof the means (or process) is here in this. Hence I am called Hermes Trismegist, having the three parts of the philosophy of the whole world. (Cf. notes 22 and 99 for two worldly triumvirates and their alchemical allegorizations.)

That which I have said of the operation of the Sun (i.e., the *Astral Light*, note 10) *is accomplished & ended.*

22. At Lucca on the River Serchio, Julius Caesar, Pompey, and Marcus Licinius Crassus formed the First Triumvirate, a coagulation

of principles occasionally understood in medieval alchemy as allegorical code for the *tria prima* of Paracelsus (see note 129). Lucca therefore came to symbolize the cosmos as a whole.

As the ideal cosmos was considered coextensively coterminous with Christendom, it was found fitting to furnish the city with the *Volto Santo di Lucca*, a wooden effigy of Christ on the cross, carved firsthand from life (rather, death) by none other than Saint Nicodemus. This worthy man (apparently prosperous, perhaps by alchemical expedient) has a role in the Gospel of the above-mentioned John of Patmos, as follows:

> *And there came also Nicodemus, which at the first came to Jesus by night, and brought a mixture of myrrh and aloes, about an hundred pound weight. Then took they the body of Jesus, and wound it in linen clothes with the spices, as the manner of the Jews is to bury.*
> —John 19:39-40

Of great significance to our poem, extra-canonical sources state that Nicodemus also stuffed and staunched the nail holes, thorn abrasions and spear wound with stalks and blossoms of *verbena* (see passim).

> *Qui non ha luogo il Volto Santo!*
> *qui si nuota altrimenti che nel Serchio.*

> (Here the Volto Santo has no place!
> Here you swim otherwise than in the Serchio!)
> —*Inferno*, Canto XXI

23. There are three Fates: Clotho, spinning the life-yarn; Lachesis, measuring out the length of that thread; and Atropos, snipping

the fiber at death. But, in our context, there is one more textile entity who looms in our poet's future, to make a fourth as Uriel does among the triad of canonical archangels (see note 205).

Like Eliot's countable but unidentifiable shade (see note 29: *I don't know whether a man or woman*), the fourth fate cannot be seen where he/she lurks in his/her modest lower apportionment, acquiescing to a subsidiary role, gliding nondescript in unisex *mantle and hood*. While draped in a transvestite burka of pudency, at a moment's notice he/she can be rung down like a curtain on the poet's career, or swathed like *lilac gauze* to render more alluring the outlines of his *long-pronged hongpronged / Underhanded baby-fetcher.*

24. *limb upon extraneous limb*

Cf. lines 436-8: Saraswati, Lakshmi, Parvati and a couple of other polymeliacal Hindu deities.

25. *Silence is the universal refuge, the sequel to all dull discourses and all foolish acts, a balm to our every chagrin, as welcome after satiety as after disappointment...*
—Thoreau

26. Flavio Vettorelli, the famed Milanese geomancer and second cousin-in-law of the present annotator, in courageous defiance of the International Astronomical Union, did his own calculations of the pertinent polar coordinates, both real and azimuthal, and demonstrated that the distance between Lourdes Grotto and Saint Jean Chapel in Tarbes corresponds, almost down to the centimeter, with that between the church of Mostar and the hill of Podboro, near the birthplace of Nikola Tesla. (See note 46.)

Furthermore, Il Sig. Vetorelli has discovered that Lourdes International Airport lies between the latitude of Saint James Church in Medjugorje and the latitude of the peak of Krizevac Mountain, even deeper in Tesla country, where the Blessed Virgin has been granting apparitions nearly as profitable as those vouchsafed to Saint Bernadette in the aforementioned Pyrenees tourist trap.

27. *wedded-hardly-bedded…sanctified princesses*

The U.S. National Lourdes Pilgrimage Office is promoted by the Knights of Columbus. These anti-Freemasons, loyal catechumens of practitioners of pedophile priestcraft, arrange for gaggles of disabled children to visit the grotto where they can be exposed to the cynical blandishments of the *sanctified Queen* of Heaven, who manifests there, often announcing her advent by *scent*. (Cf. line 375 and accompanying note for a further olfactory Marian apparition, She of the Roses.)

One day Columbo and his men
They took and went ashore
Columbo sniffed around the air
And said, "I smell a whore" [emphasis added]
And ere they'd taken twenty steps
Among the Cuban jungles
They found King Bolo & his queen
A-sittin' on their bungholes…

One day Columbo and the queen
They fell into a quarrel
Columbo showed his disrespect
by farting in a barrel. [emphasis added]
The queen she called him horse's ass

And "dirty Spanish loafer"
They terminated the affair
By fucking on the sofa
—T.S. Eliot, *Inventions of the March Hare: Poems 1909-1917*

If the barrel Columbo farts into can be taken as the queen's metonymzied nose (the logical place to aim flatulence, for full offensive effect), then it can be assumed, taking Aristophanes' *Peace* for a guide (warranted in a poet who produced an *Aristophanic melodrama* of his own, however fragmentary), that Colombo also *fingered the queen* in contravention of our poet's admonition (see line 195).

HERMES:
...And that's a hoe maker there...He's just farted in the face of that sword maker.

TRYGEAS:
And see how happy that man is? He's a maker of sickles. He just stuck his finger up at the spear maker!
—Aristophanes, *Peace 546-9*

By farting, fingering and fucking her, Eliot is expressing not only his contempt for the occult (see note 42 on "Madame Sosostris"), but his Anglican disdain for Mariolatry, virulent as can be expected in a convert. This he does in the person of "Columbo," bringer of syphilis back from the New World.

The science of physiognomy tells us that an elevated sense of smell, along with proportional development of the pertinent facial feature, would be expected in a queen who precedes herself with scent. Eliot published Rudolf Kassner, his generation's foremost writer on that science, in the *Criterion*, and visited him in Paris, where they surely would have discussed the magisterial work of Joseph Simms:

We may recognize a high degree of Olfactiveness when we see a long, sharp, straight nose; and the reason of this is not difficult to discover or far to seek. This kind of nose indicates a great surface for the operation of the olfactory nerves; and in the increase of strength with length, it bears a striking resemblance to the telescope, the reaching powers of which are increased in the ratio of the increase of the length of the inner barrel [emphasis added] *surface. The longer and larger is the instrument—granting, of course, that it is otherwise constructed on the requisite scientific principles—the greater the power of reach: and in like manner with the nose—the longer and wider the nostril the greater is the olfactory surface, and the more fully developed is the faculty of Olfactiveness.*
—Joseph Simms, M.D., *Physiognomy Illustrated, or Nature's Revelations of Character: A Description of the Mental, Moral and Volitive Dispositions of Mankind, as Manifested in the Human Form and Countenance (1887)*

According to Simms, hypertrophy of septum and nares indicates Levantine ethnicity, which in this case would entail a contradiction of received critical opinion. For, though encountered in Cuba, in tandem with black King Bolo, Eliot's queen has long been taken to represent Isabella I of Castile, and Columbo's rough treatment of her as sublimating a client's resentment of his patron. But the physiognomists carry the day in this case. It is the Israelite Virgin who must be called the first true Queen of All Iberia. When that peninsula was still a Roman province, she appeared in Zaragoza to the elder of the Boanerges (see note 44: *kosher Dioscuri*).

This was the first of all the countless thousands of Marian apparitions in the subsequent twenty centuries, and kicked off the requisite visitations by *fair and glorious ladies* to virtually all western alchemists of post-antiquity, their "nymphs" and "sibyls" only being labeled such to lend the mystique of classical scholarship. (See above and below, passim.) This gaseous female is in fact an elemental spirit disguising herself with the images already in seers', saints' and adepts' minds (see note 95). Her category of entity has been known to hang around single locales for all of recorded history, so the mere millennium and a half that transpired between James and "Colombo" would be a lark.

If Proust's evocative cookie can be named after the proverbial prostitute, there's no reason why the special hogo of the sex worker can't conjure the Blessed Virgin. From a literary standpoint, a certain scurrilous school of critics have long insisted that, whether she be intended to represent Mary or Isabella, this *smelly whore* who America's discoverer *fucked* on the *sofa* was directly modeled on Eliot's first wife. (Cf. note 73 for Aldous Huxley's appraisal of Vivienne Haigh-Wood Eliot's aroma as determined by her addiction to snorted ether.) Parallels have also been suggested with the nasally fixated Veronica of the Cross, in particular with regard to that seeress' impaired health (cf. note 95). Vivienne's symptoms included not only hyperolfaction, but inflammation of the colon and rectum, otherwise asymptomatic elevation of body temperature, fatigue, insomnia, migraines with phonophobia, and insanity outright.

In private correspondence, Eliot admitted, "I am very dependent upon women (I mean female society)." If Vivienne did indeed serve as Eliot's muse for the March Hare poems, it might provide a Neoplatonic explanation for what some critics (the present annotator excepted) perceive as a decline in quality in comparison to the rest of his work:

> *What oracle can ever be produced from distempers of the body?...Does not the worthless trance happen at the same time with debility?... Of all things, do not compare diseases of the body, such as suffusions, and fancies set in mo-*

tion by morbid conditions, with the divine vision…. The presence of the daemons weighs down the body and chastens it with diseases….
—Iamblichus, *Theurgica, or On the Mysteries of Egypt*

Blavatsky's vampire moon, Adam's Lilith, Nabokov's dwarf Kali, and Christ's woman with menorrhagia are examples of feminine entities who come with intentions of draining rather than conferring vitality. (Cf. notes 106, 120 and 138.) Unfortunately, the majority of manifesting Blessed Virgin Marys fall into this category, diocesan protestations to the contrary notwithstanding.

28. This is nothing less than the Root Tone of Nature. Adepts, prophets, mystics, alchemists, and, above all, poets have always heard it. Elijah was privy to the "still small voice" when he hiked Horeb (1 Kings 19:12). To Matthew Arnold's ear was vouchsafed the "eternal note of sadness" as he combed Dover Beach.

A city of any time or nation, if situated far enough away to be apprehended as a whole, produces this *cosmic note*: the same sung by a river in full springtime spate, or a vast deciduous forest when the wind rushes through its boughs. It is said to occupy the wavelength of F above middle-C on a piano well-tempered and tuned precisely to A at 440 hertz.

> *Hast thou attuned thy heart and mind to the great mind and heart of all mankind? For as all Nature-sounds are echoed back by the sacred River's roaring voice, so the heart of him who in the stream would enter must thrill in response to every sigh and thought of all that lives and breathes.*
> —*Book of Golden Precepts* (trans. Helena Petrovna Blavatsky)

It has ostensibly been crooned by at least one Italian anal sphincter (see note 27).

29. *feckless third*

The Waste Land has it thus—

> *Who is the third who walks always beside you?*
> *When I count, there are only you and I together*
> *But when I look ahead up the white road*
> *There is always another one walking beside you*
> *Gliding wrapt in a brown mantle, hooded*
> *I do not know whether a man or a woman*
> *—But who is that on the other side of you?*

—to which that particular poem's learned annotator replies,

> *The...lines were stimulated by the account of one of the Antarctic expeditions (I forget which, but I think one of Shackleton's): it was related that the party of explorers, at the extremity of their strength, had the constant delusion that there was one more member than could actually be counted.*

Shackleton himself contributes this:

> *...at school ... literature consisted in the dissection, the parsing, the analysing of certain passages from our great poets and prose-writers ... teachers should be very careful not to spoil [their pupils'] taste for poetry for all time by making it a task and an imposition.*

It becomes clear that the *feckless third*, who intrudes on the Poet and his love, who with subliminal yammering drowns out the *cosmic note*, who is sensed but unseen at the bottom of the page, is none other than the present learned annotator, the *fourth fate* (see note 23). He/She *dissects, parses and analyzes,* but, it is to be hoped, does not descend to *remarkable expositions of bogus scholarship* or *licentious free-association.* (Cf. notes 48 and 52.) And, like Paracelsus (but unlike a certain jolly, tinkering modernist), if he/she be accused of *bombast,* it is only by the uninitiate and the vulgar.

30. *behind—or far ahead*

See note 1 for the present annotator's special idiolection of prepositions of space. Such utter three-dimensional vertigo is as essential as *contrasexuality* itself (cf. note 99) to the mystery in which our poet is being initiated:

> *...Ye men unto whom it belongeth to hear, hearken to that which I shall declare unto you at this especial time as I hang here. Learn ye the mystery of all nature, and the beginning of all things, what it was. For the first man, whose race I bear in mine appearance, was born head downwards....He, then, being pulled down—who also cast his first state down upon the earth—established this whole disposition of all things, being hanged up an image of the creation, wherein he made the things of the right hand into left hand and the left hand into right hand, and changed about all the marks of their nature, so that he thought those things that were not fair to be fair, and those that were in truth evil, to be good. Concerning which the Lord saith in a mystery: Unless ye make the things of the right hand as those of the left, and those of the left as those of the right, and those that are above as those below, and those that are behind as those that are before, ye shall not have knowledge of the kingdom.*
> —Acts of Peter, xxxviii

31. *And why beholdest thou the mote that is in thy brother's eye, but perceivest not the beam that is in thine own eye?*
    —Luke 6:41

To which the apocryphal Saint Peter would have to reply, "Which eye?"

32. *the woman you were destined to become?*

Our poet, Eliot on his mind, his poem ridden by that *tempting demon and evil angel*, while believing himself to be addressing his fair and glorious lady, betrays his unconscious equation of the true "feckless third" (i.e., the present annotator) with *The Waste Land*'s transgendered "personage": the *old man with wrinkled female breasts*. (Cf. note 137 for Siegfried Tolliot's eschewal of silicone implants.)

> *Tiresias, although a mere spectator and not indeed a "character," is yet the most important personage in the poem, uniting all the rest.*
> —Eliot's note

33. This is a formulation from *A Subtle Allegory Concerning the Secrets of Alchemy, Very Useful to Possess and Pleasant to Read*, by Michael Maier. A Rosicrucian, his *fair and glorious lady* (see note 1) came in the guise of the Erythraean Sibyl, named Herophyle, also known as the Gentile Maiden. Rather more shy than Christian Rosenkreutz's muse, she did not boldly accost Maier from behind—nor even from the side, as our poet's gnostic Sophia has done (see note 13)—but upon Maier's own frontal approach withdrew into the shadows of her Red Sea cave. From among the stalagmites she schooled him in the alchemical secrets of the red Phoenician bird (see note 35).

34. For the female who lags behind a step or two, the re-reader is directed *back* and *above*, all the way *up* to our *Chymical* subtitle and the end note appended thereto.

35. *Or trapped in amber...*

> *Nor is Europe without her marvels....On the coasts of Prussia, a transparent and pellucid stone* [amber], *formed out of subterraneous vegetable juices, is cast ashore in large quantities....Hence Europe (the gold of the universe) seemed the very place in which I should be most likely to hear of the Phoenix and its Medicine. But most of those whom I met laughed at my quest, and said that,* like Narcissus, I had fallen in love with the shadow of my own mind....
> —*A Subtle Allegory Concerning the Secrets of Alchemy, etc.*

36. *snares...hearts*

Thales commenced his meditation on mutability by rubbing together the lodestone and amber, ἤλεκτρον (ēlektron, later adopted by George Johnstone Stoney as the name for a negatively charged particle). Attraction resulted without any change to the objects that caused it. So the lodestone and the amber must have life, and therefore souls, leading to the inevitable conclusion:

> *[Thales] held that there was no difference between life and death. "Why, then, don't you kill yourself?" someone asked. "Because there is no difference," he replied.*
> —Diogenes Laertius *I. 22*

He concluded, like the most atomistic Jaina ascetic in the deepest Hindustani jungle, that all things are full of gods. Like insects in *amber*, gods inhere:

> *Pantheists…reject the idea of a carnalized God but…perceive the divine essence in each atom. The whole world knows that Buddhism recognizes neither a God nor Gods. And yet* [for] *the Arhat…each atom of dust is as full of Swabhavat (plastic substance, eternal and intelligent, though impersonal) as he is himself….*
> —Helena Petrovna Blavatsky, "The New Cycle," *La Revue Théosophique*, March 21, 1889

37. *scarring innocent hearts…Missing nothing but words peopled with words*

In the most grotesque Pauline sense, the "scarring" and "missing" are to be taken literally, as with septal myomectomy or cosmetic trimming of the earlobes:

> *Ye stiffnecked and* uncircumcised in heart and ears [emphasis added], *ye do always resist the Holy Ghost: as your fathers did, so do ye.*
> —Acts 7:51

Cf. line 752 for the fallen angels' introducing artificial beautification to the daughters of men, and note 80 for Siegfried Tolliot's recourse to the more common form of this category of body modification.

38.   *Great in the council, glorious in the field*

This is one of the most widely applied formulaic epithets in the oral-improvised *Iliad*. Patroclus in particular is assigned these two ostensibly admirable qualities. The only unambiguous male in our own epic's long catalogue of apparitions (apart from Prince BOR-NOGO of line 878), Patroclus materializes posthumously before Achilles. He has come to sue for a proper cremation so his shade can enter Hades—that wrongheaded realm of the imagination, where Universal Logic and Justice, in the form of probation, have been eternally suspended for most souls. Alongside Eliot, Patroclus, killer of no fewer than fifty-three human beings, seems to embody—rather, to *dis*embody—Blavatsky's *tempting Demon, the evil angel, the inspirer of all our worst deeds.*

39.   *long red thread…climbed the fence before me*

The previous line's ruffling of the *Iliad*'s pages affords an opportunity to allegorize the behavior of our poet and his lover with the war of extermination the Jews waged in Canaan, itself an Homeric roman-a-clef, according to the *licentiously free-associative* if not *bogus scholarship* of yesteryear:

> *Gerardus Craesius, in his* Homerus Hebraus sive Historia: Hebraorum ab Homero, *maintained that the history of the Israelites, till their complete subjugation of Judaea, is plainly narrated in the two poems; that the Odyssey was written first, and embraces the time from the departure of Lot out of Sodom, to the death of Moses; and that in the* Iliad *is contained the destruction of Jericho, together with the wars of Joshua and the conquest of Canaan….*
> —Edward J. Goodwin, *Miscellaneous Notes and Queries, Volume 12, 1894*

Between the doomed double walls of Jericho resides the harlot Rahab, a cooperative provider of intelligence and furtive ingress and egress. She binds the famous *long red thread* in her window, signal-wise, that she might live and eventually become the great-great-grandmother of King David.

In the process she saves her family from the genocidal *herem* ban, ordered by jealous YHWH, which entails Israelites slaughtering every man, woman, child, baby, ox, donkey, puppy, etc., as they tend to do with any inconvenient ethnicity that interferes with settlement.

> *Now go and smite the Amalekites, and utterly destroy all that they have, and spare them not; but slay both man and woman, infant and suckling, ox and sheep, camel and ass.*
> —1 Samuel 15:3

But, of course—

> *...all the silver, and gold, and vessels of brass and iron, are consecrated unto the Lord: they shall come into the treasury of the Lord.*
> —Joshua 6:19

To disappoint any expectation that flirtation or banter might enter into the dealings between crack Israeli shock troops and a beautiful prostitute, their bargain is expressed in the most unerotically legalistic terms:

> *And it shall be, that whosoever shall go out of the doors of thy house into the street, his blood shall be upon his head, and we will be guiltless: and whosoever shall be with thee in the house, his blood shall be on our head, if any hand be upon him. And if thou utter this our business, then we will be quit of thine oath which thou hast made us to swear.*
> —Joshua 2:19-20

The bargain being struck, the Jews *climb the fence,* which is our poet's delightfully reductive way of phrasing a successful siege that left the fortifications in a sorry state.

> *I know that the LORD has given this land to you and that a great fear of you has fallen on us, so that all who live in this country are* melting [emphasis added].... *When we heard of it, our hearts* melted [emphasis added]...
> —Joshua 2:9-11

(See note 7 for the dissolving effects of weaponized white phosphorus on the human body.)

40. *your light summer dress*

Cf. note 7: *dressing for the ball.*

41. *ancestors wielding scimitars…dangling from a lone quince…singing in a cloud of flies*

Surprisingly, given the Eliotian context, this is not the "arbitrary" and multi-mythical figure to be found in that poet's note, as follows:

> *The Hanged Man, a member of the traditional pack, fits my purpose in two ways: because he is associated in my mind with the Hanged God of Frazer, and because I associate him with the hooded figure in the passage of the disciples to Emmaus in Part V. The Phoenician Sailor and the Merchant appear later; also the "crowds of people," and Death by Water is executed in Part IV. The Man with Three Staves (an authentic member of the Tarot pack) I associate, quite arbitrarily, with the Fisher King himself.*
> *—The Waste Land*

Rather, our entomological nimbus arrives courtesy of a single, discrete, corporeal and vividly historical *singer* whose ancestors *wielded* literal *scimitars*:

> *"This then is my story. I have re-read it. It has bits of marrow sticking to it, and blood, and beautiful bright-green flies."* [emphasis added]
> —*Lolita* (1955, Paris)

No less than Nikola Tesla in Colorado (see note 46), this *re-reader* engaged clouds of Rocky Mountain lepidoptera. When in Utah, Nabokov netted his *Eupithecia nabokovi*—not a bright green fly, but a mousy-colored moth, and by no means the specimen discovered later in the Grand Canyon, as follows:

> *I found it and I named it, being versed*
> *in taxonomic Latin; thus became*
> *godfather to an insect and its first*
> *describer — and I want no other fame.*
> —"On Discovering a Butterfly"

(Cf. note 138 for a *bogus scholar*'s misidentification of this insect.)

Is this tetralingual entomologist, perhaps, an alternative embodiment of the Poet whose entrance has been anticipated by the foregoing step-wise descent of Creators, Demiurges and Tinkers in their diminishingly divine manifestations? He bears flies, whose larvae are the very avatars and penultimate agents of physical dissolution; but his art, his *story*, has made them *beautiful*, and caused them to radiate the most propitious hue of the transcendent Tablet (see line 45).

The emerald glow of his bright-winged spondees leave no doubt that this Poet, and perhaps other Poets as well (including the one presently undergoing annotation), in spite of—or perhaps due to—their carnal corruptibility, are permitted to treat of *materials prime and ultimate*, as follows:

> *In* Gods of a Ransacked Century *Marc Vincenz gives us a full cosmology, with a broader sweep than the Hebrew Qabala's stone-plant-beast-man-angel-god. Kicking things off with a "flurry of non-dimension" lasting a billionth of a second, he wastes no time delving right into the* materia prima *of old alchemical specs. (Cf. note 129.) Tachyon-waves coagulate into atoms; molecules grow double. Shiva's formative* Lasya *commences with the "taunting belly dance of cells diversifying within light and water." Next, the "viral ice" of a meteor panspermatozoically seeds our "life-blessed world." Teeth and claws swell to spears; arrows exacerbate into bullets and hydrogen bombs, and so forth. And, just in the nick of time, we come to the finer evolutionary elaborations that Marc Vincenz is most loved for: the gastronomic and erotic. "Rocket salad with artichokes and bacon, that superb Sauvignon Blanc '88" are delectated, of course, by women. Like lightning bolts discharging in primordial soup, Marc Vincenz' women quicken their creator's* materia prima. *The end result, as always in his books, is a further flowering of his generation's finest love lyrics.*
> —Gods of a Ransacked Century (back cover), Unlikely Books 2013

42. *fraudsters…flick of a card*

> *Madame Sosostris, famous clairvoyante,*
> *Had a bad cold, nevertheless*
> *Is known to be the wisest woman in Europe,*

With a wicked pack of cards. Here, said she,
Is your card, the drowned Phoenician Sailor,
(Those are pearls that were his eyes. Look!)
—*The Waste Land*

Thus does our poem's *tempting demon*, whose self-portrait is the hyperphallic Jolly Tinker, blaspheme the Mighty and Ineffable Pythoness of Dnepropetrovsk—on shaky ground (cf. note 48). He takes his cue from his castigator (sometimes euphemized *editor*) Ezra Pound, who formulated for Blavatsky this most insultingly reductive of all possible epithets: *the Gertrude Stein of the occult.* Cf. note 180 for that *occult Gertrude Stein's* appraisal of the *dreaded magnetism* exuded by ginger-headed men, such as Pound himself.

(See below, passim, for more on the *Cantos'* maker.)

43. *Siegfried Tolliot*

This, of course, is the pseudonym of the "electronic broadcast medium" and "digital alchemist," who gained notoriety in the late nineteen-seventies with history's most widely perceived evocation of an elemental spirit, effected by means of coast-to-coast live television, specifically a guest appearance on the National Broadcast Company's *Today Show*, during which the anchorwoman was flattened and stupefied on her personal Damascus road.

A poetic treatment of the escapade has been supplied to the present annotator via private email message from Panguitch Community College in Nevada. The eponymous hero of the semi-autobiographical epyllion is simultaneously a self portrait and an homage to Eliot's "Jolly Tinker in heat."

Morningtime sloshes along the hot landmass
of Abraham Lincoln from right to the left.

Hebrew ass-backwards, like citrus juice
just violated with vodka it sloshes,
till everything's steely and orange.

A saffronish crust vaguely chipped from the crotches
of one quarter-billion times two sets of eyelids
wafts downward on omelets both fried and neglected
in anticipation of Bare-Naked Dinkus Boy.

He squats in the Manhattan green room
rehearsing fatidical leers, while Anchor-girl Pauley,
purblinded by Klieg light, unable to simper,
like old Saul of Tarsus, can flatulate nothing
but vapid, dead air....
—excerpt from *Bare-Naked Dinkus Boy Meets Jane Pauley* (unpublished manuscript)

(See *Afterword.*)

44. *lockets...plumed heirlooms*

Siegfried Tolliot has been famous for this type of accessorizing ever since the winter of 1958, when he briefly sojourned at Saint Elizabeth's Mental Hospital in our nation's capital. There, at the hands of an all but defunct federal government agency, he underwent a chemically induced auto-epiphany, as follows:

The Office of Services known as "Strategic,"
though dwindled since Hitler to straggling fanatics,
ensconced in a chamber next door to the pharmacy,
tested truth serums on schizoids and maniacs,
rapists and pedophiles, girls with Tourette Syndrome,
plus the occasional androgyne sweetheart
(yours truly, bedungeoned in sad falsity).

Scopolamine, mescaline, chased with a soupçon
of warm paregoric, made Bare-Naked Dinkus Boy
laugh off his cage, whose bars were my ribs,
whose lock was my character, previously foetal....
—excerpt from *Bare-Naked Dinkus Boy Meets Jane Pauley*

The serumic truth revealed to Tolliot was prototypically *alchemical* in that it induced the materialization of a feminine spirit (see above and below, passim). But, rather than ambushing him from behind or blasting out of a tree's split trunk (cf. notes 1 and 153), this entity coalesced from protoplasm and blood gases already seething inside his corporeal alembic. This led to Tolliot becoming an unsung pioneer in the then-embryonic American transgender movement. He "turned Tiresias" several months before glamorous Christine Jorgensen. And so was born the eponymous hero of Tolliot's unpublished epyllion.

In selecting a label for his particular psycho-physio-sexual identity, Siegfried Tolliot had recourse to a term from Greco-Roman antiquity: *priapic eunuchism*. This entails removal of the testes but not the penis (*i.e.*, the Eliotian *long-pronged hongpronged / Underhanded babyfetcher*). Thus is conserved what he has since dubbed his "boner energies" in honor of the Jewish Castor and Pollux ("Boanerges," cf. note 89). Tolliot's particular variation on the kosher Dioscuri makes them conjoined twins of the *dicephalic parapagus* variety. Paradoxically, this effect was achieved by the surgical extirpation of a subset of "twins," resulting in a compound entity Tolliot has called *Castrato and Bollocks*. Many traditions on both sides of the River Don preserve male gonads for later reunification in the gelding's afterlife. To the same end do the sons of Hirohito tote their salted umbilical cords in little wooden boxes from cradle to crematorium.

From the tambourine I have eaten.

From the cymbal I have drunk.
I have borne the cup of gonads.
The room I have entered.
—Firmicus Maternus

The *room* Tolliot *entered* was the "schizy ward" in the Washington, D.C., insane asylum. And the most notorious application of his conserved "boner energy" took place in conjunction, as it were, with that ward's most glamorous inmate, Ezra Pound. (See line 308, *kissing my bristly chin,* and accompanying note.)

Cf. line 890, *unto the shrine of the most obscene god,* for a similar lower-digestive ritual conjuring an altogether more horrific spirit in the Algerian Sahara.

45. Newton's dog, Diamond, was the discoverer of pathologically exceptionable theorems, and burner of twenty years' worth of experimental notes.

To Newton and to Newton's dog Diamond, what a different pair of Universes; while the painting on the optical retina of both was, most likely, the same!
—Thomas Carlyle, *The French Revolution: A History*

See note 21 for his master's translation of Hermes Trismegistos' *Tabula Smaragdina.*

46. *battery-powered eyes*

In such a Nabokovian context (see below, passim), the notion of flickering eyes brings inevitably to mind the defensive spots on butterfly wings that mimic in relative giantism those organs of sight.

So great was the power being thrown out by Tesla's "magnifying transmitter" that light bulbs within one hundred feet of the station glowed regardless of whether they were connected to any circuit and all the electrical equipment of a nearby fuel company ceased to function....Even the insects felt the effects of the electrical barrage. Butterflies became electrified and helplessly swirled in circles —their wings spouting blue halos of Saint Elmo's Fire.
—Harry L. Goldman, "Nikola Tesla's Bold Adventure." *American West (1971).*

Cf. note 26 for Marian geomancy's Teslaic nuances, and note 131 for the Serbian electrician's ostensible contribution to the development of Father Marcello Pellegrino Ernetti's astounding *Chronovisor*, through which several of our poem's historical personages are seen to behave and heard to speak.

47. *"Before these events...later will vanish"*

Cf. note 51 for the esoteric language of the birds.

...the Antichrist returns for the last time.... All the Christian and infidel nations will tremble...for the space of twenty-five years. Wars and battles will be more grievous than ever. Towns, cities, citadels and other structures will be destroyed..... So many evils by Satan's prince will be committed that almost the entire world will find itself undone and desolated. Before these events many rare birds will cry in the air. "Now!" "Now!" and sometimes later will vanish.
—Nostradamus, Epistle to Henry II

48. *I am not familiar with the exact constitution of the Tarot pack of cards, from which I have obviously departed to suit my own convenience.*
    —*The Waste Land*, note 46

Eliot enjoyed a similar level of expertise, and took proportional liberties, with the teachings of *Madame Sosostris*, all in the name of padding out his *chef d'oeuvre*, as follows:

> *…it was discovered that the poem was inconveniently short, so I set to work to expand the notes, in order to provide a few more pages of printed matter, with the result that they became the remarkable exposition of* bogus scholarship [emphasis added] *that is still on view to-day.*
> —*Frontiers of Criticism*

It remains one of literature's more peculiar displays of autoerotic masochism, this poet subjecting his own work to bogus scholarship. There has never been a shortage of other *critical frontiersmen* (and -*women*) ready to impose it from without. (Cf. lines 555-6: *I daren't speak my name aloud / for fear Kali would hear me,* and the accompanying note on Nabokov's *dwarf Kali*.)

49. *Cities, walled cities…raw fingers leaving her bloody trace…primal scream booming through walls*

Cities of God, any god, tend to have such faithless fortifications, even those built by ethnicities YHWH has deemed worthy of extermination. We have returned to Jericho. (See note 39.) One forgets that genocide and vandalism usually entail sacrilege as well:

> *As the early masons knew, the plans of the earliest cities were never arbitrary or utilitarian but in strict accordance*

with sacred doctrines.... Thus the founding itself was a religious act wherein the site was chosen according to an oracle consulted or an auspicious sign offered by a sacred animal or a flight of birds.... In the words of Livy: "There is not a place in this city which is not impregnated with religion."
—Helen Valborg, "The City," *Hermes Magazine*

The *bloody traces, nightly blazes* and *primal screams* are results of the divine *herem* ban.

50. *mumbled incomprehensibly*

Cf. note 170 for Dr. John Dee's Enochian syllables of invocation.

51. *Most wonderful is that kind of Auguring of theirs, who hear, & understand the speeches of Animals, in which as amongst the Ancients, Melampus, and Tiresias, and Thales, and Apollonius the Tyanean, who as we read, excelled, and whom they report had excellent skill in the language of birds: of whom Philostratus, and Porphyrius speak, saying, that of old when Apollonius sate in company amongst his friends, seeing Sparrows sitting upon a tree, and one Sparrow coming from elsewhere unto them, making a great chattering and noise, and then flying away, all the rest following him, he said to his companions, that that Sparrow told the rest that an Asse being burdened with wheat fell down in a hole neer the City, and that the wheat was scattered upon the ground: many being much moved with these words, went to see, and so it was, as Apollonius said, at which they much wondered.*
—Heinrich Cornelius Agrippa: *Of Occult Philosophy, Book I,* Part iii

52. *Hatless!*

Except for *shtreimlech, kippot,* and certain black fedoras, hats were removed from American men's heads by a certain savior arche- type, who paradoxically owed fealty to the Jew-hating Vatican. This Jesus figure, though uncrowned with thorns, did die of pub- licly inflicted wounds, whose blood was stanched, at least meta- phorically, with the same member of the vegetable kingdom that was applied to the original Christ's nail holes after crucifixion. (See note 22 on *verbena*.)

By all the accounts of senators, Supreme Court justices and NAACP bigwigs who were granted audiences with our thirty-sixth presi- dent while he eased nature on the flush commode adjoining the Oval Office, LBJ's *underhanded babyfetcher* coincidentally shared many of verbena's physical properties: the hairy, hardy blossom, lavender color, thick stalk, etc. In private email correspondence with the present annotator, Siegfried Tolliot claims to see a "pro- found connectivity" between this "anatomical synchronicity" and Lyndon Johnson's behavior on the plane from Dallas, as described by an understandably put-off former First Lady:

> *That man was crouching over the* [hatless] *corpse, no lon- ger chuckling but breathing hard and moving his body rhythmically. At first I thought he must be performing some mysterious symbolic rite he'd learned from Mexicans or Indians as a boy. And then I realized—there is only one way to say this—he was literally fucking my husband in the throat. In the bullet wound in the front of his throat. He reached a climax and dismounted. I froze. The next thing I remember, he was being sworn in as the new pres- ident.*
> —Jacqueline Kennedy Onassis, interviewed by Paul Krassner in "The Parts That Were Left Out of the Ken- nedy Book," *The Realist*, Issue Number 74, May 1967

Tolliot derides as "licentiously free-associative" the school of thought, current in certain far northern Nevadan academic circles, that draws a connection with Ezra Pound's (and the entire English-speaking world's) most famous haiku—

In a Station of the Metro
The apparition of these faces in the crowd;
Petals on a wet, black bough.

—whereby the instrument of JFK's cervical desecration becomes the *wet bough*, symbolically *blackened* by LBJ's championing of the Civil Rights Movement. As Tolliot points out, this would have turned the stomach of our poem's *tempting demon*, whose own cycle of Colombo poems inspired "In a Station of the Metro." The obvious anachronism needn't be discussed in a cosmic dispensation that recognizes time's Einsteinian untensefulness. (See note 18.)

On the "schizy ward" of Saint Elizabeth's Mental Hospital, in 1958, Tolliot lifted a sheaf of theretofore unpublished correspondence from Ezra Pound's nightstand, which yielded just barely enough academic fodder to garner him lifetime employment in a remote, far-northern Nevada community college. This previously unexamined document, with learned annotations subtended by Tolliot himself, appeared in the *Kanorado Review of the Collective Humanities* (*KrotCH*), since defunded and rendered defunct by the Coordinating Council of Literary Magazines and Presses for the offense of rejecting one of their minor apparatchiks' prose poems.

With this pilfered text, Siegfried Tolliot made simultaneous contributions to the fields of Eliot and Pound studies. It solved a mystery long debated in Poundian circles by revealing the poet's debt to Eliot for the subject matter of the foregoing haiku, in a reversal of the pattern of influence those two poets had established. It turns out that Pound's overworked *petals* are dense, hairy purple verbena blossoms, evoking syphilis chancres more vividly than the usually suspected pale Japanese cherry petals. The botany as well as the epidemiology is clarified by Pound's admission of derivation from the following Colombo fragment:

> *King Bolo's swarthy bodyguard*
> *Were called the Jersey Lilies*
> *A wild and hardy set of blacks*
> *Undaunted by syphilis.*
> *They wore the national uniform*
> *Of a garland of verbenas*
> *And a pair of great big hairy balls*
> *And a big black knotty penis.*

On the immediate biographical level, the haiku turns out to be Pound's account of exposing his penis (wishfully rethought as *wet* and *black, big* and *knobby*) to a platform full of "wops" in the town of Predo as they boarded one of the trains that Mussolini had caused to run on time.

> *I don't care how you spell your wop painters, and I don't know whether* [Ambrogio de Praedis] *was from Predi, Predo or Predis. Never been to his home town.*
> —letter to Carlo Izzo, 1938

(Cf. note 167 and *Afterword* for Tolliot's regular visits to Pound's hometown in a presumably "professional" capacity.)

> *Came not by usura Angelico; came not Ambrogio Praedis,*
> *came no church of cut stone signed: Adamo me fecit.*
> —Canto XLV

One of the few strictly autobiographical poems Pound ever wrote, and the most ill-advised, "In a Station of the Metro" was taken as evidence in the sanity hearing that landed him in Saint Elizabeth's Insane Asylum to be burgled, so to speak, by the likes of Tolliot. (Cf. line 237: *Don't become the narrator of your own life.*)

53. Melville's *Ishmaelite* protagonist is evoked. (Cf. note 4.)

54. *bleating porpoises*

When our poet causes us to hear these cetaceans with humanoid intelligence making the noise of proverbially stupid sheep, he intends to remind us of Blavatsky's—

> ...*spirits of one or another element...combinations of sublimated matter and rudimental mind...centers of force having instinctive desires but no consciousness as we understand it...unable to invent anything...automatically reflecting stamped impressions in the human memory... having neither developed will nor intelligence...hence tending automatically to copy forms of higher beings...*

Swathing themselves in the most numinous fabrics that can be snuffled, dog- or hog-wise, from among our brains' involutions, they appear resplendent, but are only capable of parroting the insipidities tucked like mothballs among the gloried tissues. The average human mind is capable of storing more impressive visual than verbal effects. See passim for such doltish dolphins masquerading and babbling as *Blessed Virgins, pole star nymphs,* and alchemically *fair and glorious ladies.*

Beckett's "Ping" holds a certain clinical interest as a depiction of possession by one of these bleating porpoises who blurt what they find in the mind of the energumen. In this case, the percipient is in such a state of intellectual enervation that the revelation can only be expressed in rudimentary terms approaching Dr. Dee's barbarous syllables in meaninglessness. (Cf. Note 170.) A pitch of despair has sunken deep enough to strip any vestiges of spirituality away, even at the basic visual level that entertains these dog-like entities.

The moronic repetition of the word "white" is significant, as if the babbler (whose gender, among almost every other marker of individuality, has been minimized away) is arrested at the leucotic stage of Jungian alchemy: the *albedo*, in which animus and anima blur without discrimination. (See passim for numerous and various contrasexual eunuchs and hermaphrodites.)

> *...Head naught nose ears white holes mouth white seam like sewn invisible over. Only the eyes given blue fixed front light blue almost white only colour alone uncover. Light heat white planes shining white one only shining white infinite but that known not. Ping a nature only just almost never one second with image same time a little less blue and white in the wind. Traces blues light grey eyes holes light blue almost white fixed front ping a meaning only just almost never ping silence. Bare white one yard fixed ping fixed elsewhere no sound legs joined like sewn heels together right angle hands hanging palms front. Head naught eyes holes light blue almost white fixed front silence within. Ping elsewhere always there but that known not. Ping perhaps not alone one second with image same time a little less dim eye black and white half closed along lashes imploring that much memory almost never. A far flash of time all white all over all of old ping flash white walls shining white no trace eyes holes light blue almost white last colour ping white over...etc., etc.*

55. *an aging man who writes to me from time to time*

Briefly, and uniquely in the entire poem, our poet does this humble scholar the inexpressible honor of assuming his/her voice. See Afterword for Tolliot's pestering emails triggering the present annotator's spam filter.

56. *noted professor of anthropology*

Namely Siegfried Tolliot. See Afterword for his precious and prideful emeritus professorship. It's not in anthropology at all, but rather a squalid and loathsome pseudo-discipline whose designation has been suppressed at this early point in our primary text in deference to *re-readers'* stomach contents, and to postpone the audience attrition so inevitable in a work of this specialized category.

An Eliotian context can be expected to ignore an Audenian directive:

> *... Thou shalt not sit*
> *With statisticians nor commit*
> *A social science.*
> —from "Under Which Lyre: a Reactionary Tract for the Times"

57. Contrary to reports, Socrates could not have been an Eleusinian initiate because, ridden by his famous nay-saying daemon, he lacked the requisite psychic integrity. How many other *Socratic fellows* wander about our agora? Professor Emeritus Tolliot with his inner Bare-Naked Dinkus Boy qualifies. Oppenheimer, ridden by no less an entity than Shiva (see note 112), was allowed access to the atomic mysteries, with appalling results.

58. In a poem where the syzygy of Christ has just murmured in his ear as he stood facing death in Palestine, our poet could be soliloquizing: *Hypocrite lecteur, — mon semblable, — mon frère!*

59. *Fingering* seems to be the least portion of the treble outrage perpetrated against Eliot's fragrant sovereign. (See note 27.)

Tolliot is one figurative "queen" who poetically *self*-fingers. He writes in a self-devised system of dactyls (which he alternately describes as "rough" or "intermittent" or "throbbing") to emphasize the priapic nature of his eunuchism: he is *fingered* in the same way that Wotan is *un*-fingered. (Cf. lines 211-14.)

> *...metri dactilici prior intrat syllaba, crebro impulsu quatiunt moenia foeda breues....*

> *The first syllable of the dactyl, the long, represents the penis, and the two short syllables the testicles.*
> —J. N. Adams, *The Latin Sexual Vocabulary*

This trope exploits a vulgar prosodical-physiological pun of long standing:

> SOCRATES
> *Plague seize the dunce and the fool! Come, perchance you will learn the rhythms quicker.*

> STREPSIADES
> *Will the rhythms supply me with food?*

> SOCRATES
> *First they will help you to be pleasant in company, then to know what is meant by enhoplian rhythm and what by the dactylic.*

STREPSIADES
Of the dactyl? I know that quite well.

SOCRATES
What is it then, other than this finger here?

STREPSIADES
Formerly, when a child, I used this one.

SOCRATES
You are as low-minded as you are stupid.
—Aristophanes, *Clouds*

60. *Icelandic wool…maddening other*

In the *Nibelunglied*, Brunhild, queen of Iceland, denies her hymen
to the king on their wedding night. Only by the breaking of her
bones is she persuaded to behave like a proper wife. Unlike Lilith
of a fundamentally opposed tradition, Brunhild is not replaced by,
but is turned into, Eve (Aryan style). Still caged within the bounds
of this housebroken spouse's skeleton is her *maddening other*. The
mother of demons must be *fended off*.

61. *woman kept…goddess revered…careful distance, afar*

No contradiction here: cf. *I smell a whore*, note 27.

62. *The king…thin and frayed*

In Wagner's version of this, based in part on the Icelandic Poetic
and Prose Eddas, Wotan, king of the gods, is avid for the titu-

lar ring, but never gets it. Hence he's depicted metonymically as *lacking a pointing finger*, which is the digit of potency, the index, upon which Royal and Papal symbols are placed. He is in a state of decrepitude because there remains nothing for him to do in this godly twilight but to set Valhalla on fire and die.

63. *infernally mumbling…living grave*

In a masterful subordinate clause, our poet effortlessly forces this dead king of the gods to undergo a rebirth ten thousand times more degrading than anything Wagner could imagine in all his titanic perversity. Uproariously to salt the wound, the reincarnation is done by Mishnaic means. (Cf. notes 11 and 147 for *embryonic coercion*.)

Wotan returns as Alberich, avaricious chief of the contemptible Nibelungen dwarves, subterranean scrapers of symbolically fecal wealth from the earth's intestines, such as one hundred-percent carbon diamonds to be *schlepped* to Belgium for *farkoif—*

> *My house is a decayed house,*
> *And the jew squats on the window sill, the owner,*
> *Spawned in some estaminet of Antwerp….*
> —T. S. Eliot, "Gerontion"

Once again opposites have been morphed, if not reconciled. Currency speculation, offshore banks, hedge funds (cf. lines 344-5): Alberich does the work of the unmanned, or at least those whose manhood has been clipped. This paradox is apropos, for the eunuch in our poem who collected interest ("CONTRA NATURAM," see note 80) from the author of "With *Usura*," was of the priapic variety. At this point, the "finger" the king retains is by no means the index. One has become two, the *babyfetcher* has doubled. (Cf. note 17 and lines 387-90.)

We will see that our poet in this case resists subsumption. By his very nature, amply, doubly, triply sexed, he's no Nibelung, and knows nothing of such glittering debasement. Cf. lines 413-16.

64. *A mortal lives not through that breath that flows in and that flows out.*
     The source of his life is another and this causes the breath to flow.
     —Paracelsus

We first met our poet when, having been *damned straight to Gaza*, he was on the verge of getting not only his eyes, but his life white-phosphorized away. His fair and glorious lady, in the guise of the Southerly wind, insufflated him and *caused his breath to flow*. She is the *other* who constitutes the *source of his life*.

65. *"Do not become the narrator of your own life!"*

Cf. note 52 for the cautionary tale of a major modernist who failed to take this advice and paid for it with incarceration in the insane asylum.

66. *measure the long days*

According to Einstein's untenseful formulation, such calibration would be redundant in any case. But, for a voyeuristic work-around, see Father Marcello Pellegrino Ernetti's *Chronovisor*, note 131.

67. *frescos of history willfully recorded*

Looking back on our first canto's tour of Rome, Babylon, Knossos (but not Jerusalem): see lines 15-25.

68. A hinted recapitulation of *eyeless Samson on his pillar* (see note 4), in preparation for an imminent manifestation of similarly blind Aldous Huxley. Like Eliot with his *Jolly Tinker* and Tolliot with his *Bare-Naked Dinkus Boy*, Huxley will clothe himself in borrowed poetical garb. (Cf. line 284.)

69. Captive Samson feigns orientation. As usual, our prepositions of space are rendered arbitrary by blindness, i.e., *pretense*. (Cf. notes 48 and 52, respectively, for *bogus scholarship* or *licentious free-association*.)

70.   *That houre as Phœbus issuing foorth, did bewtifie with brightnesse the forhead of Leucothea, and appearing out of the Occean waues, not fully shewing his turning wheeles, that had beene hung vp, but speedily with his swift horses Pyrous & Eous, hastning his course, and giuing a tincture to the Spiders webbes, among the greene leaues and tender prickles of the Vermilion Roses, in the pursuite whereof he shewed himselfe most swift & glistering, now vpon the neuer resting and still moouing waues, he crysped vp his irradient heyres.*
        —Francesco Colonna, *Hypnerotomachia Poliphili (Poliphilo's Strife of Love in a Dream)*

    Cf. note 17 for an Eliotian rendering of this celestial phenomenon, with demiurgic overtones.

71. *spurned or seeded*

    Again, in this context, there is no contradiction. The *or* in this phrase appears in place of *and* merely by convention. The psycho-drama upon which our poet has embarked is webbed, warped and woofed with antitheses.

72. Marlowe, *Edward II*.

73. *antic hay*

Clothed in Marlowe's pentameter, Aldous Huxley seems to make his entrance, deceptively affable in the guise of an early comic novel. But he has been subliminally with us since Canto One, middle-aged orbits cauterized, myopic as Milton:

> *...Promise was that I*
> *Should Israel from Philistian yoke deliver;*
> *Ask for this great deliverer now, and find him*
> Eyeless in Gaza *at the Mill with slaves....*
> —*Samson Agonistes*

It's a work from Huxley's old age that more completely informs our poem: The *Devils of Loudon* is full of astral doings and elemental attacks on women's physical and psychical integrity. But why does Huxley come unnamed, disguised under other poets' works? His attitude toward the works of our *tempting Demon*, our *"evil angel"* might be one cause:

> *...the marriage in* The Cocktail Party *was inspired—*
> *if that is the word—by Tom's own marriage. His wife,*
> *Vivienne, was an ether addict, you know, and the house*
> *smelled like a hospital. All that dust and despair in Eliot's*
> *poetry is to be traced to this fact.*
> —comment to Robert Craft

Cf. note 27 for Vivienne as Elliot's olfactory muse, and note 95 for Saint Mary of the Roses performing the same aromatic service for Veronica of the Cross.

74. This is the simultaneous threat, and promise, of Buddhist eschatology, in particular the *Shambhala* vision, as reconstituted by the venerable Chögyam Trungpa, teacher of Allen Ginsberg, who appears in our poem as both literal and figurative embodiment of both poles of this metempsychotic precept, including the idiomatic usage that pertains to mental health. (Cf. note 80.)

75. To the Greeks and Romans, Provence had its provenance with the Ligures, who misnamed themselves, according to Plutarch, being ignorant of their own origins.

> *Their country is savage and dry. The soil is so rocky that you cannot plant anything without striking stones. The men compensate for the lack of wheat by hunting.... They climb the mountains like goats.*
> —Posidonios

Their country may have been short on *antic hay*, but that did not stop them from *dancing*. They even looked like *goats*:

> *...Ligurian tribes, now shorn, in ancient days*
> *First of the long-haired nations, on whose necks*
> *Once flowed the auburn locks in pride supreme...*
> —Lucan, *Pharsalia*

76. *trout...white wine...Senses awaken*

A characteristic moment for this most sublimely culinary of living poets—

That chilling kindness, rocket salad with artichokes and bacon, that superb
Sauvignon Blanc '88, the way your eyes diamond even when your husband
is in earshot...
—Marc Vincenz, "Pinatas and Clowns," *Gods of a Ransacked Century* (Unlikely Books, 2013)

This is a demonstration, if one were needed, that our poet has resisted being transformed into a gold-nibbling dwarf.

77. *corrupted vessel*

> *It came to pass on a time that matter conceived a desire to attain to the superior region; and when it had arrived there, it admired the brightness and the light which was with God. And, indeed, it wished to seize on for itself the place of pre-eminence, and to remove God from His position. God, moreover, deliberated how to avenge Himself upon matter, but was destitute of the evil necessary to do so, for evil does not exist in the house and abode of God. He sent, therefore, the power which we call the soul into matter, to permeate it entirely. For it will be the death of matter, when at length hereafter this power is separated from it. So, therefore, by the providence of God, the soul was commingled with matter, an unlike thing with an unlike. Now by this commingling the soul has contracted evil, and labours under the same infirmity as matter. For, just as in a corrupted vessel, the contents are oftentimes vitiated in quality, so, also the soul that is in matter suffers some such change, and is deteriorated from its own nature so as to participate in the evil of matter. But God had compassion upon the soul, and sent forth another power, which we call*

Demiurge, that is, the Creator of all things; and when this power had arrived, and taken in hand the creation of the world, it separated from matter as much power as from the commingling had contracted no vice and stain, and hence the sun and moon were first formed; but that which had contracted some slight and moderate stain, this became the stars and the expanse of heaven. Of the matter from which the sun and the moon was separated, part was cast entirely out of the world, and is that fire in which, indeed, there is the power of burning, although in itself it is dark and void of light, being closely similar to night. But in the rest of the elements, both animal and vegetable, in those the divine power is unequally mingled. And therefore the world was made, and in it the sun and moon who preside over the birth and death of things, by separating the divine virtue from matter, and transmitting it to God.
—Alexander, Bishop of Lycopolis, *Of the Manichæans,* Chapter III: "The Fancies of Manichaeus Concerning Matter"

78. *man in Mycenae*

Agamemnon, sacrificer of Iphigenia, inheritor of Cassandra, commander of the invading force in the war over the sister of Castor and Pollux (see note 89), is the only man who ever had more truck than an alchemist with prophetesses, demi-goddesses, fair and glorious ladies, and troublesome succubi.

79. *She's withered…apart from the tree*

Cf. Lines 604-6 for Cyliani's tree-splitting pole-star Nymph. Now before our eyes she puckers into the Blessed Virgin Mary in Anatolian retirement. She shrivels into the tantric crone by whom the gag reflex is transgressed, serving the same function as smoking corpses on Ganges ghats perform for Aghori mendicants. (Cf. note 171.) The Mother of Christ, in her forties when at the *tree* (her son's gallows), was twice that age when The Beloved Disciple installed her next door to the Temple of Diana at Ephesus.

80. *kissing my bristly chin*

Our poet momentarily assumes the beleaguered persona of Eliot's *castigator* (cf. note 42). The kiss is being planted not by Siegfried Tolliot but a far more glamorous fan who has already appeared, above, in the context of *mind loss* and *personality disintegration* (see line 287).

Allen Ginsberg may have been Chögyam Trungpa's humblest pupil (see note 74), but he was Ezra Pound's most assiduous stalker. He actually beat Tolliot to the Poundian punch at Saint Elizabeth's. The prototypical beatnik had been "forgiving" Mussolini's former propagandist for decades. It's not been widely publicized, but the twentieth century's most famous instance of poetical osculation, in Venice, on Pound's eightieth birthday, was in fact a *re*-kissing.

Such is well-known among poetic insiders. But here it can be revealed for the first time, via private email correspondence, that the stalker had a stalker of his own. Tolliot showed up in the "schizy ward" on the rounded heels of the author of *Howl* after the latter had orally primed the old native Idahoan. In his quality as Bare-Naked Dinkus Boy, posing as a candy striper, the priapic eunuch put himself into a position to lend Ezra Pound a carton of Kool mentholated cigarettes—good as dollars in any locked-down sanitarium. The lender took advantage of the borrower's senility to extract an unreasonable rate of interest, to be taken out in services rendered.

> *...with usura,* sin against nature... [emphasis added]
> *It hath brought palsey to bed, lyeth*
> *between the young bride and her bridegroom*
> *CONTRA NATURAM...*
> —Canto XLV

The copulatory details are, frankly, too sordid to bear repetition in these brief annotations. Suffice it to say that, in preparing to "use the patient as Christ did The Maiden" (cf. line 421: *Goodnight, John*), the offender got his own *long-pronged hongpronged / Underhanded babyfetcher* circumcised—which, in adults, even those sans testes, is no minor surgical procedure, often involving general anaesthesia.

> *Thus saith the Lord GOD; No stranger, uncircumcised in heart, nor uncircumcised in flesh, shall enter into my sanctuary, of any stranger that is among the children of Israel.*
> —Ezekiel 44:9

No doubt owing in part to increased sensitivity of Tolliot's unprepuced glans penis, his scheme was carried out, his escapade encompassed, with dispatch, so that the guards and male nurses (also plied with Kools) could claim no notice. (Cf. note 103 for *ejaculatio praecox* in the *Book of Revelation*.)

> *The diagnosed schizophrenic was heard to quote his deceased protege from beneath the clanking institutional bed:"He's come to fuck us all,"*
> —private email correspondence with the present annotator (Cf. note 17.)

Tolliot refers to his behavior in the "schizy ward" at Saint Elizabeth's as *pulling a Lot's daughter.* The Bare-Naked Dinkus Boy used the anti-Semitic poet's dementia precisely as those middlingly Asiatic versions of Aemilia and Licinia (see note 2) used their father's drunkenness in the Adullam cave (Genesis 19:30-38):

> *Indeed I lay with my father last night; let us make him*
> *drink wine tonight also, and you go in and lie with him,*
> *that we may preserve the lineage of our father.*
> —Genesis 19:35

This indicates not only Tolliot's obvious transsexual quasi-Electra complex (shared by any number of neutered postmodern poetasters), but, more historically important, his sense that, in our time of literary croneyism and critical degeneration, Pound's poetic *lineage* needed *preservation*. And, from Tolliot's point of view, there could be no better way to ensure that preservation than through the Bare-Naked Dinkus Boy's verse. The Tolliotian dactyls only began to "throb" after engagement (so to speak) with the author of the *Cantos*. Pound can be said to have *fingered* Tolliot in return, in the sense of equipping him with the long syllable and the two short that touched off his *boner energy*. (See note 44.) As in the case of Dr. Ripley's alchemical king with low sperm count and poor motility, a burrowing into the parental orifice was required to promote fecundity. (See line 768 and accompanying note.)

81. *Still there is a child within.*

In Canto One of this poem about embryogenesis, our poet was olfactorily fecundated by the Southerly wind. The zygote impends within his inseminated cranium, and constitutes our poem.

> *They said that Athena was the daughter of Zeus not from*
> *intercourse, but when the god had in mind the making*
> *of a world through a word (logos) his first thought was*
> *Athena...*
> —Justin Martyr

*...he represents Athena as mind (νοῦς) and intellect
(διάνοια); and the maker of her name seems to have had a
similar conception of her, but he gives her the still grander
title of "mind of God" ἡ θεοῦ νόησις...*
—Plato, *Cratylus* (407B)

For another instance of autoparthenogenesis, cf. note 105: Swee'
Pea's immaculate dam, Olive Oyl, and her quasi-terpsichorean
role in the deduction of the double helix.

82. *Hair slips from its bun...white upon hot white*

This is the inevitable transformation into the tantric crone, which
even the Blessed Virgin underwent in Ephesus, here expressed in
Medusa's terms. Cf. line 425: *the propensity of getting old.*

83. *Comprehend* is used in the sense of *encompass.* Tiresias has penetra-
ted himself in his own act of autoparthenogenesis.

84. Perseus is heard talking here via the technical expedient of the
Chronovisor. No tantric initiate, the son of Danae would rather
not suppress his gag reflex and engage the hag. He has his own way
of dealing with her, using an adamant blade forged by Hephaestus
(a.k.a. Vulcan: cf. note 19), and a bronze shield of similar divine,
if low-tech provenance, burnished to reflectivity.

85. Marlowe, *Hero and Leander.*

In cases where their isolation is symptomatic of some deeper un-
wholesomeness, these *lone women* can become seeresses and open
their psychic doors to astral company, more often than not to the

detriment of their health. (Cf. note 95 for the valetudinarians Vivienne Haigh-Wood Eliot and Veronica of the Cross.)

In the Second Sestiad of the same epyllion, the solitary lady is about to receive a visitor in the form of aural insufflation, as our poet did in Canto One:

> *And now she lets him whisper in her ear,*
> *Flatter, entreat, promise, protest and swear…*

Cf. note 13 for Marlowe's appraisal of this method of conception as practiced on the Blessed Virgin Mary.

86. What birth can be so numinous, or baneful, as to cause the knees to buckle? Skull-delivered Athena, or the cinematic spawn of Anton LaVey? (See notes 81 and 171, respectively.)

87. *I catch myself…seething, steaming*

Whatever the character of this fresh abortion-Christ child, the shock of its appearance affects our post traumatically-stressed poet no less drastically than Rosemary's baby did Mia Farrow. (See line 375.) Vincenz is sent spinning through a Gazan flashback to the "War" of 2008-9, as reflected in the novelty-style lineation. The re-reader is urged to take up his *derriere garde*.

88. *idle chatter*

See Israel Regardie on the efficacy of barbarous syllables of invocation (note 170).

89. *John...James*

At this late stage in the terminal decay of monotheism, any mention of the "Boanerges" or "Sons of Thunder" brings to mind Castor and Pollux, spawn of pagan Zeus. The earlier pair of siblings having been permitted to sit on the left and right hand of their god, John and James requested the same consideration from their Master, and got rebuked for it, as follows:

> *...the sons of Zebedee came unto him, saying, Master, we would that thou shouldest do for us whatsoever we shall desire. And he said unto them, What would ye that I should do for you? They said unto him, Grant unto us that we may sit, one on thy right hand, and the other on thy left hand, in thy glory. But Jesus said unto them, Ye know not what ye ask...*
> —Mark 10:25-40

Hellenized Jews could be relied upon to leap back and forth from the Homeric epos to the Koine gospels with unconscious ease. Going among polyglot modernists as we've been, a similarly effortless leap of logic and faith into scriptural Joyceanity is not unwarranted:

> *...remember ham to me, when we were like bro and sis over our* castor and porridge [emphasis added], *with his roamin I suppose...*
> —*Finnegans Wake*

Joyce's mangling of the second name takes us to another brace of brothers, one of whom had an inordinate fondness for *porridge*, as follows:

> *And Jacob sod pottage: and Esau came from the field, and he was faint: And Esau said to Jacob, Feed me, I pray thee,*

with that same red pottage; for I am faint: therefore was
his name called Edom. And Jacob said, Sell me this day
thy birthright. And Esau said, Behold, I am at the point
to die: and what profit shall this birthright do to me? And
Jacob said, Swear to me this day; and he sware unto him:
and he sold his birthright unto Jacob. Then Jacob gave
Esau bread and pottage of lentiles; and he did eat and
drink, and rose up, and went his way: thus Esau despised
his birthright.
—Genesis 25:29-34

—which leads us straight back to the more pertinent modernist
we've been dealing with all along, our poem's *tempting demon,* and
his views on Britain selling its birthright (its young men) for a very
messy mess of *porridge:*

Perhaps you are tempted to give them a picture of a leprous
earth, scattered with the swollen and blackening corpses
of hundreds of young men. The appalling stench of rotting
carrion, mingled with the sickening smell of exploded lyd-
dite and ammonal. Mud like porridge, *trenches like shal-*
low and sloping cracks in the porridge—porridge *that*
stinks in the sun. Swarms of flies and bluebottles cluster-
ing on pits of offal. Wounded men lying in the shell holes
among the decaying corpses: helpless under the scorch-
ing sun and bitter nights, under repeated shelling. Men
with bowels dropping out, lungs shot away, with blinded
smashed faces, or limbs blown into space. Men screaming
and gibbering. Wounded men laughing in agony on the
barbed wire, until a friendly spout of liquid fire [em-
phasis added] *shrivels them up like a fly in a candle. But*
these are only words, and probably only convey a fraction
of their meaning to their hearers. They shudder and it is
forgotten.
—T. S. Eliot, letter to *The Nation*

Cf. *This Wasted Land*'s first canto for the politicidal use of white phosphorous outside the hallowed boundaries of Christendom.

No stranger to *bowels* and *gibbering* in his role as "Castrato and Bollocks," Siegfried Tolliot extends our John and James trope deep into the blind sac of post-modernity.

90. The Templars, dwarfed and castrated by the Inquisition, having formerly burrowed like Nibelungen under Herod's temple rubble and scraped up mineral treasures to hoard and lend *with Usura*, (cf. note 80), took secret refuge in Helvetia, and taught the yodeling natives all the crass money-grubbing pursuits our poet proudly disdains in lines 413-16.

91. Ben Jonson, *The Devil Is an Ass*

The same accusation of asininity, made against Queen Elizabeth's co-religionists, brought Jonson's friend Christopher Marlowe to the attention of the Star Chamber:

> *That if there be any God or any good religion, then it is in the Papists, because the service of God is performed with more ceremonies, as elevation of the mass, organs, singing men, shaven crowns, etc. That all Protestants are hypocrit-ical asses.*
> —Richard Baines' note to the privy council, listing Marlowe's blasphemies

See notes 13, 94, 104 and 192 for further clauses in this shocking indictment.

92. Here our poet is approached by the Woman who is far from *little*,

just as Christian Rosenkreutz was approached by his fair and glorious lady, John Dee by his Daughter of Fortitude, Cyliani by his Pole Star Nymph (see note 153), Crowley by his Ape of Thoth, Jack Parsons by his Babalon, *etc.*

93. Jennifer Jones, who starred eponymously in *Song of Bernadette*, was born on the day of the eldest Fatima seer's death. That year Boston got flooded with molasses, in the sort of synchronicity whose pertinence the occult mind apprehends instantaneously as the remembrance of a Proustian madeleine.

94.   *That if Christ would have instituted the sacrament with more ceremonial reverence, it would have been in more admiration; that it would have been better much better being administered in a tobacco pipe.*
      —Richard Baines' note tattling on Marlowe to Queen Elizabeth's privy council

95. In occult circles it is widely known that the film's eponymous heroine (gotten with child by supernatural means) is named allegorically after Saint *Mary* of the *Roses*, who revealed herself to Veronica of the Cross on the day of theatrical release.

   As it entailed olfaction, the apparition was named after the flower. This answers to the movie, in which a charm necklace is given the percipient, containing a fictional strong-smelling root, fancifully named for the Nile delta city from among whose bulrushes baby Moses was pulled by Bithia, Pharaoh's daughter (Midrash Leviticus Rabbah 1:3)—no doubt significant in a yarn spun by someone named Ira Levin.

   Both the film and its exactly contemporaneous Marian apparition offer textbook cases of manifestation involving, not an alchemist-seer, but a mediumistic seeress, specifically of the Popish confession, whose morbid transubstantial theophagy tends to attract carnivorous rather than numinous elementals. (Cf. note 36 for Madame Blavatsky on *carnalized* gods.)

Like Eliot's spouse Vivienne, Veronica of the Cross suffered extensive physical dissolution. One of the most beautiful women of her time and place, she quickly degenerated into a horrific specimen, bloated and bent, with eyes red and distended from staring for days without a blink into the delusive *blue sky* (see note 10). With a tumor on the spine, granulated vertebrae, heart attacks requiring deployment of wheelchair and oxygen tanks, and, of course, the menorrhagia universal to these cases (cf. note 138 for the *woman which had an issue of blood twelve years*), Veronica of the Cross ended up a premature embodiment of the crone whose sheer physical grotesquery qualifies her for the sacred role of tantric initiatrix. (See note 171.)

Any center of consciousness compelled by the Vatican's formulaic gyrations would only be clothed, as it were, to resemble something formerly human, draping itself with such regrets and desires as could be absorbed from the medium's avid, fervid brain. Like so much that is theistic, Our Lady of the Roses was every bit as blackly magical in fact as Anton LaVey's cameo role was in fiction: a lurid burlesque of Vama Marga tantrism in self-deluded disguise, a barely camouflaged modification of the more sordid workings in the *Clavicula Salomonis Regis* (See note 163).

A counterfeit elemental in disguise, of course, this constantly re-appearing Mary can hardly be who she claims, the personality (with rare exceptions) crumbling to nothingness soon after the corpse. Only the most devout papists entertain the possibility of the Blessed Virgin's unsmutched carcass having been divinely assumed in A.D. 40.

We have a *bleating porpoise.* (See line 180.)

> *They will search the memory to its very depths. Hence the*
> *nervous exhaustion and mental oppression of certain sen-*
> *sitive natures...*
> —Helena Petrovna Blavatsky, *Isis Unveiled*

And hence the seemingly psychosomatic haematomata of the hands and feet suffered by Veronica and almost every other Mariolatrous seeress over the past two millennia, along with a slit of spontaneous hemorrhage and peritonitic fluid between a certain pair of floating ribs, and extravasation of serum from thorn-shaped lesions on the forehead.

96. Cf. notes 13 and 164 for the significance of lateral sidling in our poem's astral *Weltanschauung.*

97. *One becomes two...one as fourth*

This is a further arithmetic extension of Eliot's *long-pronged hong-pronged / Underhanded babyfetcher,* as calculated by the methods of Maria Prophetissa, the reputed inventrix of such essential chymical kit as the *tribikos, kerotakis* and *bain-marie.*

Among Arabian scholars she was known as "Daughter of Plato." But the western tradition was compelled to call her "The Jewess," as in Europe the Arabian epithet denoted sulfur, the alchemical principle that binds a substance to its transformation through flammability (cf. note 129). It is, of course, coincidental that The Jewess should be next-door-neighbor, on the Periodic Table of Elements, to a particularly horrific substance, the military application of which, in our first canto, is effecting politicide in a "strip" abutting a unilaterally disengaged Israel.

See also lines 605-6 for Cyliani's tree-splitting Nymph, a projection from the pole star, who revealed the formulation: *From one by one which is only one are made three, from the three two, and from the two, one.*

Elsewhere in *This Wasted Land*, quartets are made of the normally triple Fates and canonical archangels: see notes 23 and 205, respectively.

98. *she looks younger...stripes*

Cf. note 165 for *striae distensae's* unpuckering, as the tantric transgression of the gag reflex is chastened. Decrepitude is reversed at will in an Einsteinian anti-temporal dispensation.

99. *Egyptian queen...Nile*

The Second Triumvirate was the political alliance of Octavian, Marcus Aemilius Lepidus, and Marc Antony. Whereas the First Triumvirate came to allegorize Paracelsus' Three Primes (cf. note 129), this later trio represented the three alchemical stages, originally four, as follows:

1. *Nigredo* (blackening or *melanosis*) was personified by Octavian, who, in his quality as Augustus, initiated the *Pax Romana*, which corresponds to the seeming inactivity of the base material prior to commencement of the Great Work.

2. *Albedo* (whitening or leucosis) was assigned to Marcus Aemilius Lepidus—

...a slight, unmeritable man,
Meet to be sent on errands...
—*Julius Caesar*, 4:1:13-14

After pledging loyalty to the Senate, he flipped to Marc Antony's camp, showing weakness of character reminiscent of the envious, sick and pale moon (see line 424), as seen by the alchemical imagination prior to Madame Blavatsky's revelation of that satellite's horrific character. (Cf. note 106.)

And yet, Marcus Aemilius Lepidus' errand-boy behavior enables the Magnum Opus to commence, as his *leucosis* sucks up to Marc Antony's—

3. *Citrinitas* (yellowing or *xanthosis*).

After the fifteenth century, the latter was combined with—

4. *Rubedo* (reddening, purpling, or *iosis*)—

—to make the three stages that answer to the Second Triumvirate. This is reflected in the mingling of Cleopatra (*iosis*) with Marc Antony (*xanthosis*), in a typically Egyptian conception of hermaphroditic individuation. In the Jungian system, which restored the quaternity, Antony and Cleopatra together comprised the *albedo*, in which animus and anima combine contrasexually. (See passim for numerous and various contrasexual hermaphrodites.)

100. A Helvetian "miracle" that generates endless polyvinylchloride profit for the Swiss patent-holder, the epitome of artifice and artificiality, yet for all that an honest act of biomimesis, inspired by something natural as burrs on a biodegradable spaniel's fur, Velcro serves in our poem as the transitional material that fastens the hedge funds of crass bankers in Bern to Alpine thickets where *rabbits breed / and wild birds lay speckled eggs*. (See note 90 for Templars in Switzerland.)

101. Cf. note 104 for the psychoanalytical implications of sado-masochistic scopophilia.

102. Our poet puts hedge funds and similar Nibelungery in their place.

103. *He which testifieth these things saith, Surely I come quickly. Amen. Even so, come, Lord Jesus.*
    —Revelation 22:20

    I come quickly is repeated in the seventh, twelfth and twentieth verses of John's Apocalypse, the same number of times the corresponding refrain is heard in this canto. The assurance of Revelation is here turned into an exhortation, expressed as the plea of a tired publican. The *ejaculatio praecox* that closes off Holy Writ becomes *postcox*, as it were. The implication is that our entire book ends here, in spite of subsequent cantos and all their formidable critical apparatus.

    Einstein's *stubborn illusion of tenseful time* (see note 18) and the re-reader's redefinition of prepositions of space in temporal terms (see note 1 and passim) are climaxed by our poem coming to its resounding close several cantos before it actually ends. The re-reader is launched into a strange limbo as with the virtuous pagans—but not before having his face shoved into the belly of the most horrifying creature in the entire Vincenzian oeuvre. (See line 423 and subtended annotation.)

104. *Goodnight John, sorry James*

    The pleasant valediction offered to the younger brother, followed by the apology to the elder, comprises a special Vincenzian prophecy of their future conditions, as registered extra-canonically, after this party has broken up.

John, who began as the youngest and ended the oldest disciple, enjoyed the longest incarnate tenure in the bosom of Our Savior. As the Beloved, a.k.a. "the Maiden," he was privileged to be used like a favored girl by the Master:

> *That Saint John the Evangelist was bedfellow to Christ and leaned always in his bosom; that he used him as the sinners of Sodoma.*
> —Richard Baines' note to Queen Elizabeth's Privy Council, containing several reports of heterodox statements by Christopher Marlowe

Due in part to this history of shared intimacy, John was privileged to weep with the three Marys at the foot of the cross, while James, along with the other cowards, *stood afar off, beholding these things* (Luke 23:49), exhibiting a passively sadomasochistic scopophilia later dissected by the father of psychoanalysis as follows:

> *Whenever we find in the unconscious an instinct of this sort which is capable of being paired off with an opposite one, this second instinct will regularly be found in operation as well. Every active perversion is thus accompanied by its passive counterpart: anyone who is an exhibitionist in his unconscious is at the same time a voyeur; in anyone who suffers from the consequences of repressed sadistic impulses there is sure to be another determinant of his symptoms which has its source in masochistic inclinations.*
> —Freud, *Three Essays on the Theory of Sexuality*

On Golgotha, as a reward for his uncanny ability to maintain comparative psychosexual health in such a deviant milieu as Jerusalem, John was given charge of everyone's subsequent model of the fair and glorious maiden, the Queen of Heaven, the Woman Clothed in the Sun, et al. He installed her in Ephesus for her retirement in the shadow of the temple of her multi-dugged counterpart. (Cf. note 164 for the alchemical Nigredo's extra breasts.) There, in her post-menopausal state, Mary became the tantric crone, Galilean-style, yet with her spring-loaded hymen remaining a virgin, in spite of having whelped Christ and his numerous siblings (Matthew 13:53-57).

John went on to writer-in-residency on scenic Patmos, where he composed the valedictory bits of Holy Writ, Christendom's most famous, if not accomplished, act of poetic percipiency, followed by a glorious martyrdom via boiling olive oil in Rome.

Meanwhile, the other half of the Boanerges fared less auspiciously. James' comrades got to go forth and make disciples in Italy, Scythia, Cappadocia, Armenia, Assyria, Egypt, and even India. But this other Son of Thunder never made it out from under the shadow of Jerusalem's temple—except for one brief and entirely mythological missionizing trip to Zaragoza, Spain, where, according to strictly local lore, his brain and body were subjected to a Marian apparition. (Cf. note 95 for the horrific rigors associated with that privilege.) James died in Jerusalem before the apostles could first convene in 49 A.D., and he'd been disemboweled already more than half a century by the time his younger brother wrote his Apocalypse. Put to the sword by Herod Agrippa, James' blood was left to puddle and be diluted by white phosphorous pissing disgracefully down from the sky.

105.   *Goon-night*

The slurring enunciation of a drunk and exhausted reveller, heard at the end of the party, supersedes the triple plea to Christ.

This is the first half of the most horrifying couplet our poet has ever written, for it invokes, in her most bestial form, a harpy of planetary proportions: *Alice the Goon*, a cretinous and immensely muscular she-monster who, in 1937, stalked the streets of Thimble Theater.

By no coincidence, during that signal year of 1937, a Marian apparition occurred which revealed to the seer, who happened to be a cartoonist, the greatest horror in humanity's heredity. The most twisted entanglements of our spirits in the Manichaean mire of matter were illustrated by the schematic hand of E. C. Segar, the same unconscious adept who conjured Alice the Goon. This time she appeared in her motherly aspect, in another Popeye cartoon, this one animated: *I Likes Babies and Infinks.*

Olive Oyl hugs herself in a rapture that is purely autoparthenogenetic (hence the mystery of her anachronistically swaddled offspring's nativity). She wraps her jointless arms around herself twice over—to be catalogued amongst numerous other Caduceus-braided snake images in Mariolatrous and quasi-Mariolatrous circles (*i.e.*, La Guadalupena treading upon the boa constrictor with her dainty instep).

This she encompasses in the company of her monocular lover, the very embodiment of phallicism, Penis Personified, strong as Samson but only half-blinded, his one un-popped eye symbolizing, like that of the Cyclops, the urinary meatus that surmounts the instrument of fecundation.

During the same synchronistic *annus horribilis* of 1937, the regularity of DNA's structure was revealed to William Astbury via X-ray diffraction patterns. According to received wisdom, it wasn't till some fifteen years later that Francis Crick, "The Father of Modern Genetics," intoxicated with LSD-25, hallucinated the corkscrew that made him famous. But Siegfried Tolliot has a different version, gotten at Saint Elizabeth's Mental Hospital in our nation's capital:

Deoxyribonucleically speaking,
not Astbury's patterns of X-ray diffraction
but Swee' Pea's mom wriggled and wrung
the hint Bill Crick cashed at the brainiac bank.
Neither did lysergic acid diethylamide
finagle the Father of Modern Genetics,
like some twisted Jacob, to dream up the ladder
with spiraling rungs.

This we have learned from the OSS relics
who entheogenicized Jew-baiting Ezra,
arms helixed in straitjacket-bound ecstasy,
talking the truth in serumical tonguings,
bitten like pillows and relayed to amorous
Bare-Naked Dinkus Boy, stationed in rear...
—-excerpt from *Bare-Naked Dinkus Boy meets Jane Pauley*

(See note 167 for Pound's "pillow-bite talk.")

106.   *Arise, fair sun, and kill the envious moon,*
       Who is already sick and pale with grief,
       That thou, her maid, art far more fair than she.
       Be not her maid since she is envious.
       Her vestal livery is but sick and green,
       And none but fools do wear it. Cast it off!
       —*Romeo and Juliet II, ii, 2-5*

Alchemically, the merely reflective moon represents the silver of the *albedo* that seeks transmutation by the radiative solar gold of *citrinitas*.

John of Patmos well understood this aspect of our satellite. In

Revelation 12:1-3, when the sun woman treads on the moon, she is confronted by the red dragon (*rubedo*), a glyph for the final stage of the Magnum Opus.

In Blavatsky, however, the moon is something far more sinister and sick, if not *goonish*:

> She is the satellite, undeniably, but this does not invalidate the theory that she has given to the Earth all but her corpse.... The Moon will dissolve our Earth, all its life, energy and powers; and, having transferred them to a new centre, becoming virtually a dead planet, in which rotation has almost ceased since the birth of our globe. The Moon is now the cold residual quantity, the shadow dragged after the new body, into which her living powers and "principles" are transfused. She now is doomed for long ages to be ever pursuing the Earth, to be attracted by and to attract her progeny. Constantly vampirised by her child, she revenges herself on it by soaking it through and through with the nefarious, invisible, and poisoned influence which emanates from the occult side of her nature. For she is a dead, yet a living body. The particles of her decaying corpse are full of active and destructive life, although the body which they had formed is soulless and lifeless. Therefore its emanations are at the same time beneficent and maleficent — this circumstance finding its parallel on earth in the fact that the grass and plants are nowhere more juicy and thriving than on the graves; while at the same time it is the graveyard or corpse-emanations, which kill. And like all ghouls or vampires, the moon is the friend of the sorcerers and the foe of the unwary. From the archaic aeons and the later times of the witches of Thessaly, down to some of the present tantrikas of Bengal, her nature and properties were known to every Occultist, but have remained a closed book for physicists.
> —Madame Blavatsky, *The Secret Doctrine*

To end this section of our poem with the advent of such a cosmic vampire is to express a dread that runs deeper than dreams. To name this night after the gross and goonish aspect of the demoness who harries and vampirizes the earth is terrifying. John of Patmos, contrariwise, had his Christ, the Solar God par excellence, to close off his literary composition.

With his *HURRY UP PLEASE ITS TIME* and his *Goon-night,* Marc Vincenz out-apocalypticizes the Apocalypticist.

107.   Our *sermon* needs to be *fired-up again* as it has ended so cold and ashen in the immediately previous line.

108.   *propensity of getting old*

This is a delicate definition of mortality, not necessarily needing to go unsaid among alchemists, prophets, poets, and other associates of such astral beings who populate, or, rather, *fail* to populate our poem. The self-same *fair and glorious lady* enchants and perturbs frail minds and bodies, from James Son of Zebedee to Jack Parsons, without herself showing signs of decrepitude, except illusively, when the role of tantric initatrix needs filling. (Cf. note 171.)

109.   Charybdis, once a beautiful naiad, was turned into the apotheosis of the monstrous Nigredo dream hag. (Cf. lines 671-3 and subtended note 164.) Here she is bereft of proverbially paired Scylla.

110.   *The spectral forms of the gods are uniform; those of daemons are diversified....*
      —Iamblichus, *Theurgica, or On the Mysteries of Egypt*

128

111.   Saraswati, Lakshmi and Parvati comprise the *Tridevi*, consorts of the *Trimurti*: Brahma, Visnhu and Shiva, respectively. Kali is nobody's consort, but is the all-powerful Shakti, or active principle, of Shiva.

The first three are goddesses of learning, fertility and love. The *Ganges with her corpses* might conceivably *denounce* these. But Kali can be denounced no more than gravity or entropy.

112.   *"I remembered the line from the Hindu scripture, the* Bhagavad-Gita; *Vishnu is trying to persuade the Prince that he should do his duty, and to impress him, takes on his multi-armed form and says, Now I am become Death, the destroyer of worlds."*

Oppy went on TV with that routine, pretending to try, with a more or less recondite reference, to rehabilitate himself in the philosemitic eyes of the liberal intelligentsia, when he knew very well that his perfect face had already done the job for him the moment he melodramatically averted his moony eyes from the camera.

It's not just War Department flunkies like him who have access to universally lethal knowledge. In the apocryphal Acts of Thomas, *Jesus takes his doubting disciple aside and whispers three esoteric words. When the other apostles crowd around and demand to know what the Master said, Thomas replies, "If I were to reveal even one of those words, you would take up stones to kill me, and those stones would turn to fire and burn you up."*

Every writer has just such moments. He looks up from his manuscript, his head reels, and, like Melville, he gasps, "I have written a wicked work." With Coleridge, he says of himself, "...Beware! Beware! His flashing eyes, his floating hair! Weave a circle round him thrice, And close your eyes with holy dread, For he on honeydew hath fed, And drunk the milk of paradise."

In other words, "Publish this book, big fella, and the world comes to an end." And there's not even a momentary quibble. To Hell with the world, and with me!
—Fission Among the Fanatics (Spuyten Duyvil Press)

Like Siegfried Tolliot (a.k.a. Bare-Naked Dinkus Boy), or T. S. Eliot (a.k.a. Jolly Tinker), or James Humphrey Morris (a.k.a. Jan Morris: see note 136), Oppenheimer self-transformed into a naughty antithesis, in his case, Shiva. He named history's first man-detonated nuclear explosion *Trinity*, after the Hindu *trimurti* of Brahma-Creator, Vishnu-Preserver, and Shiva-Destroyer.

Cf. note 190 for what a genuine subcontinental Brahman, unaided by crass technology, can do through the might of Shiva: the discombobulation of cause and effect, brought about by a single silent thought.

113. *Alchemy is a threefold art, its mystery well symbolized by a triangle. Its symbol is 3 times 3—three elements or processes in three worlds or spheres.... It is the number of worlds nourished by the four rivers that pour out of the Divine Mouth as the verbum fiat.*
—Manly P. Hall, *The Secret Teachings of All Ages*

114. *What has really drifted...song of the sea?*

Having in Canto One been levitated like a box kite out of the line of [al]chemical fire, our humane poet can't help but look back and wonder what fluids, what Brandtian urine blended with what liquefied flesh and boiled Ishmaelite gore, has rinsed off the Gazan pavement and into the sea. He seems to have in mind Jonathan Swift's contribution to this poetic stream:

Now from all parts the swelling kennels flow,
And bear their trophies with them as they go:
Filth of all hues and odors seem to tell
What street they sailed from, by their sight and smell.
They, as each torrent drives with rapid force,
From Smithfield or St. Pulchre's shape their course,
And in huge confluence joined at Snow Hill ridge,
Fall from the conduit prone to Holborn Bridge.
Sweepings from butchers' stalls, dung, guts, and blood,
Drowned puppies, stinking sprats, all drenched in mud,
Dead cats, and turnip tops, come tumbling down the flood.
—"A Description of a City Shower"

115. *Let it rain.*

Such a prayer for meteorological ablution does not necessarily imply a plea for peace, as in this dream of Albrecht Dürer:

In the year 1525 between Wednesday and Thursday af-
ter Whitsunday during the night I saw this appearance
in my sleep, how many great waters fell from heaven.
The first struck the earth about four miles away from me
with a terrific force, with tremendous clamour and clash,
drowning the whole land. I was so sore afraid that I awoke
from it before the other waters fell. And the waters which
had fallen were very abundant. Some of them fell further
away, some nearer, and they came down from such a great
height that they all seemed to fall with equal slowness. But

when the first water, which hit the earth, was almost ap-
proaching, it fell with such swiftness, wind and roaring,
that I was so frightened when I awoke that my whole body
trembled and for a long while I could not come to my-
self... God turn all things to the best.

116. *no testament of ancient history...clairvoyance and clarity*

Our poet has lost the recollection of the journey he took to
golden antiquity in Canto One, and the clear sight that was insufflated into his soul. Gaseous despair rushes in to supply the
vacuum in his mind, propelling him on another astral itinerary,
qualitatively opposed to the previous: a contemporary katabasis,
transported on slithering shadows rather than the personified
wind.

117. *New York...Long Island Sound*

In this infernal antithesis of his earlier paradisiacal world tour,
once again, our poet skips the so-called "Holy Land," like an
American presidential candidate flying over a squalid and backward midwestern state.

118. One of verbena's virtues. Cf. note 52.

119. *Rats big as cats...eating brains*

For Marc Vincenz as consummate gastronomic bard, cf. note 76.

120. *Nor is that worthy speech of Zeno the philosopher to be*

*passed over with the note of ignorance; who being invited
to a feast in Athens, where a great prince's ambassadors
were entertained, and was the only person that said
nothing at the table; one of them with courtesy asked him,
"What shall we return from thee, Zeno, to the prince our
master, if he asks us of thee?"*

*"Nothing," he replied, "more but that you found an old
man in Athens that knew to be silent amongst his cups." It
was near a miracle to see an old man silent, since* talking
is the disease of age; *but amongst cups makes it fully a
wonder.*

More to the point, in this age of *bogus scholarship* and *licentious
free-association*, is the less famous instance of the same memorable phrase, a few paragraphs earlier in Ben Jonson's little book of random musings, in which the active lie replaces idle yammer:

*Nothing doth more invite a greedy reader than an un-
looked-for subject. And what more unlooked-for than to
see a person of an unblamed life made ridiculous or odious
by the artifice of lying? But it is* the disease of the age....

The present annotator wishes to thank Siegfried Tolliot for, however pointedly, calling his/her attention to the foregoing passage. It's well to remind the priapic eunuch (or perhaps to inform him/her) that the inventors and past masters of such "licentious free association" were those idle punsters, the Midrashic rabbis. It is those "bogus scholars" who arbitrarily pulled Lilith out of Isaiah's ass—

*For it is the day of the Lord's vengeance, and the year of
recompenses for the controversy of Zion. And the streams
thereof shall be turned into pitch and the dust thereof into
brimstone, and the land thereof shall become burning*

pitch. It shall not be quenched night nor day; the smoke thereof shall go up for ever. From generation to generation it shall lie waste; none shall pass through it for ever and ever. But the cormorant and the bittern shall possess it; the owl also and the raven shall dwell in it; and He shall stretch out upon it the line of confusion and the stones of emptiness. They shall call the nobles thereof to the kingdom, but none shall be there, and all her princes shall be nothing. And thorns shall come up in her palaces, nettles and brambles in the fortresses thereof; and it shall be a habitation of dragons and a court for owls. The wild beasts of the desert shall also meet with the wild beasts of the island, and the satyr shall cry to his fellow; the screech owl [Lilith] *also shall rest there and find for herself a place of rest. There shall the great owl make her nest, and lay and hatch and gather under her shadow; there shall the vultures also be gathered, every one with her mate.*
—Isaiah 34:8-15

—and fastened her extracanonically on Adam's back as the Mother of All Nocturnal Emissions.

Any occasional mild forays into impressionistic analysis that might be found among the present apparatus will appear downright rigorous by the standards of those rowdy rabbis.

121. *rekindled by a fragrance or a tone...here she is again...Femme fatale de la guerre*

See passim for olfactory apparitions such as Our Lady of the Roses and King Bolo's rancid queen. (Cf. note 28 for the Root Tone of Nature.)

The *Femme Fatale de la Guerre* appears in our Mariolatrous text as the Blessed Virgin in Church Militant robes:

> *For we wrestle not against flesh and blood, but against principalities, against powers, against the rulers of the darkness of this world, against spiritual wickedness in high places.*
> —Ephesians 6:12

Margaretha Geertruida "M'greet" Zelle MacLeod, a.k.a. Mata Hari, was famous for stocking a wide array of scents in her arsenal, not every one of which was primarily olfactory in function:

> *Bouchardon ordered an analysis of the substances—soaps, creams, makeup, perfumes, and the like—in her traveling bag, hoping one would be revealed as invisible ink....*
> —Pat Shipman, *Femme Fatale: Love, Lies, and the Unknown Life of Mata Hari*

122. The knight chooses oblique angles of approach in sex and battle, not unlike more than one of our manifesting centers of consciousness, above and behind, sidling from the right, from the south, etc. But a certain orthodox rectitude is lent by the gonadal configuration of the object of Lancelot's affection, in contrast with Achilles' beloved, earlier invoked in the context of a Homeric epithet. (See note 38.)

123. The yellowness of the king's mental process recalls the penultimate stage of the Magnum Opus. *Citrinitas*, or *xanthosis*, brings about that coloration, whether in transmuting silver into gold, or replacing the merely reflective moonlight into the solar radiance of the soul's noontide. In Jung's sublimated alchemy, *citrinitas* is archetypified as the wise old man. The irony of our poet's reduction of this sublime process to a cuckolded king's invidiousness is apparent as the sallowness of skin and sclera

rendered unwholesome by liver disease.

124. These are Hennig Brandt's particular alchemical colors: his 5000 liters of yellow urine were reduced and distilled to red oil, then taken through the constellation Virgo (distillation), and finally solidified until the green light glowed.

125. *stillness…never departs*

The Root Tone of Nature can vibrate the inner ear *molto pianissimo.* Cf. 1 Kings 19:12, *the still small voice.*

126. *they stay and cradle…as Mother once did with her rock-a-bye-babies*

Such is the commonality that binds as brothers every alchemist, prophet, madman, eunuch and poet in our poem. (See passim, above and below for *dream women.*) That the *cradles* might fall, the *dreams* be bad, the *lullabies* be hissed to the tune of *Dies Irae* through the gob of a toothless hag, at this point goes without saying.

127. *Of course…chin chiseled*

This is the direct portrait of our poet's mother, singer of the foregoing *rock-a-bye-babies.*

> *Take the picture of my mother, exhibited at the Royal Academy as an "Arrangement in Grey and Black." Now that is what it is. To me it is interesting as a picture of my mother; but what can or ought the public do to care about the identity of the portrait?*

—James McNeill Whistler, *The Gentle Art of Making Enemies*

Being, like the great Whistler, a staunch adherent of *ars gratia artis*, the present annotator is aware of the ultimate irrelevance of this genealogical detail, as much as certain priapic eunuchs (see *Afterword*) delight in accusing him of "padding out his apparatus." But the fact remains that our poet has followed non-figurative Ma into the bathroom, to watch her wash in *mare's milk*, the very nutrient that almost propelled Genghis Khan deep into the moist clefts of the breast- and thigh-shaped Qionglai mountains (see line 148). With luxuriant rhyme and alliteration Vincenz delectates, even as Mother *de-lactates*, on her *china white skin* and *chiseled chin*.

Even beyond the tantric crone of the Vama Marga adepts, this is the inevitable and ultimate development of the *fair and glorious lady* who *touched us on the back in an unusual manner* at the beginning of our poem—or rather, *before* the beginning, pre-embryogenically as it were, in our very subtitle.

The re-reader will get to play the oedipal voyeur when the next logical step is undertaken, below, in the alchemical *Cantilena Riplaei*. (See line 768 and its accompanying note.) In the meantime Mama will have metamorphosed through the stages represented by Cyliani's polestar nymph, Maier's Erythraean sybil, and the papists' Blessed Virgin (see passim), finally to holometabolize into into the Imago Herself: Carnalized Mommy, with her literal vaginal canal, composed of mucous membrane and striated muscle seductively arranged over an inviting chassis of connective tissue and pelvic bone, demanding incestuously to be reverse-spelunked.

(Cf. note 13, where *Mary brought Christ into her virginity*.)

128. Cf. note 137 for Siegfried Tolliot's appraisal of one pertinent

stone carver's command of female anatomy.

129. *salts...poison*

Paracelsus' cosmos is composed of the *tria prima*: mercury, sulfur, and salt in their general spiritual principles. Mercury causes transformation through volatility and fusibility. Sulfur binds substance to transformation by flammability. Salt solidifies and fixes by lending non-combustibility.

The classic illustration of the *tria prima*, taught to all alchemical neophytes since Paracelsus' time, is burning wood. Mercury is represented by smoke, transcending the liquid and solid states, and, by extension, life/death, heaven/earth, virtue/vice, etc. Sulfur is emblematized by flame's expansion, evaporation and dissolution. Salt is seen in the base matter of ash, which contracts, condenses and crystallizes.

It's this last principle to which Siegfried Tolliot despairingly prophesies himself being reduced: see note 156, *charcoal briquettes*.

130. *Whisper of suds...drip drip drip*

Cf. note 7 for skin, whitened with suds of phosphorous, dripping off Gazan bones, and note 89 for the same phenomenon at Ypres.

131. *Stylized, heaven forbid.*

Substitute the discipline of Physics for *heaven* in this formulation, and Enrico Fermi comes to the fore, with his profound observation:

What isn't forbidden is compulsory.

While pondering the possible and therefore inevitable untensefulness of time, Fermi is supposed to have crossed paths with the eminent exorcist, quantum physicist and pre-polyphonic musicologist, Father Marcello Pellegrino Ernetti. This august cleric claimed to have collaborated with Tesla on the invention of a contraption called the Chronovisor, now buried in the Vatican vaults among doctrinally problematic Dead Sea Scrolls and theistically incorrect Nag Hammadi manuscripts.

Through the reconstruction of "luminous energy" and the filtering of harmonics (the audio portion of the Akashic record), Father Marcello's contrivance enabled him to *stand afar off*, like the elder son of Zebedee (see note 104), and peek at Christ on the cross. More importantly, the Chronovisor allowed him to view the premiere of Quintus Ennius' lost tragedy, *Thyestes*. The production, which seemed to be mounted in a senator's Palatine villa, featured not only the requisite cannibalistic consumption of sons and raping of daughters, but—even more titillatingly for a practitioner of popish priestcraft—two chorus lines of naked boys with scrota downy and dewy as verbena buds.

132. *Oxford Club*

Robert Boyle (see note 157) was a charter member.

The remainder of this stanza, and most of the next, mysterious as any lines in the voluminous Vincenzian oeuvre, seem to be viewed through Father Marcello Pellegrino Ernetti's Chronovisor.

133. The happy little hunchbacks confecting cuckoo clocks and *kirschtorte* among the Schwarzwald's hardwood oaks (long since logged into kitschy bric-a-brac and replaced with cheap conifers that are dying in their turn from acid rain) are little more than cutesified Wagnerian *Nibelungen*. But remnants of their infernal nature occasionally surface. The seven Dwarfs are briefly shown mining diamonds in the Disney cartoon. (Cf. note 63 for *schlepping to Antwerp*.)

134. *scoundrel Hapsburger…he didn't say*

These lines, tantalizing as any our poet has ever written, have withstood the present annotator's most earnest if not pedantic attempts at decoding. Scholarly conscience forfends his/her falling back on *licentious free-association*, despite Siegfried Tolliot's idle accusations (See *Afterword*).

135. *there was a woman involved, I'm certain*

This is a safe bet, in context. See passim. In the present case, the involvement is intra-corporeal.

136. *implanted me with breasts*

Jan Morris, Commander of the Most Excellent Order of the British Empire, educated at Christ Church, Oxford, who accompanied Sir Edmund Hillary and his faithful Sherpa, Tenzing Norgay, in history's first successful assault on Mount Everest, had a sex change in Morocco, more than twenty years after the blossoming forth of Bare-Naked Dinkus Boy. Unlike Siegfried Tolliot, Jan Morris was *implanted* with Michelangelic *breasts*. (See note 158.)

137. In Siegfried Tolliot's opinion (conveyed to the present annotator via private email correspondence), the artist conspicuously absent from this roll call, while a fit subject for women's cocktail party talk—

> *...carved boobies like bean bags*
> *lopsidedly stapled to bulldykish pecs*
> *on Giuliano de' Medici's steroidal tomb,*
> *where Bare-Naked Dinkus Boy*
> *learned to say "No" to surgical silicone...*
> —excerpt from *Bare-Naked Dinkus Boy Meets Jane Pauley*

He had somehow finagled a two-week "sabbatical" from Panguitch Community College, and dogged Ginsberg's steps to Venice, with the purpose of securing further Poundian sloppy seconds. While in Italy, Tolliot supposed he really ought to expose himself to the timeless treasures of Florence, if only to have something to blurt in the next faculty meeting that might for a minute or two drown out a certain colleague's perpetual droning about her "duel with Nabokov." (Cf. note 156 for *the bitch who blasphemed the bald nymphet.*)

(See note 52 for another painter missing from this roll call: Ambrogio de Praedis.)

138. *for fear Kali would hear me*

The undesirability of a destructive *shakti* hearing (and repeating) one's name is exemplified by this relatively recent instance of *bogus scholarship* and the *licentious free-association* from which it all too often issues like menorrhagia from a seeress' nethers:

In 1960, a "young lady" (as Nabokov dismissed her) published an article on *Lolita* in which she drew parallels between Humbert's paedophilia and Nabokov's lepidopteromania. She stated that the latter's most important contribution to entomology was his discovery of *Lycaeides argyrognomon (=Plebejus idas) sublivens nabokov*, which is by no means chief among his many nettings.

> *The essay by a young lady who attempted to find entomological symbols in my fiction…might have been amusing had she known something about Lepidoptera. Alas, she revealed complete ignorance and the muddle of terms she employed proved to be only jarring and absurd.*

This couldn't have been calculated to grate more agonizingly on Nabokov. He is for all time the prototypical example par excellence of fastidiousness in entomological literary criticism, as demonstrated by the following recital to the "young ladies" at Wellesley:

> *…We shall therefore assume that Gregor has six legs, that he is an insect. Next question: what insect? Commentators say cockroach, which of course does not make sense. A cockroach is an insect that is flat in shape with large legs, and Gregor is anything but flat: he is convex on both sides, belly and back, and his legs are small. He approaches a cockroach in only one respect: his coloration is brown. That is all. Apart from this he has a tremendous convex belly divided into segments and a hard rounded back suggestive of wing cases. In beetles these cases conceal flimsy little wings that can be expanded and then may carry the beetle for miles and miles in a blundering flight.…Further, he has strong mandibles. He uses these organs to turn the key in a lock while standing erect on his hind legs, on his third pair of legs (a strong little pair), and this gives us the length of*

his body, which is about three feet long. In the course of the story he gets gradually accustomed to using his new appendages—his feet, his feelers. This brown, convex, dog-sized beetle is very broad... In the original German text the old charwoman calls him Mistkäfer, *a "dung beetle." It is obvious that the good woman is adding the epithet only to be friendly. He is not, technically, a dung beetle. He is merely a big beetle....*

Nabokov's *dwarf Kali* is reputed to have been lurking in the back of the classroom during this lecture, costumed as a varsity charwoman. (Cf. Aleister Crowley's *Moonchild*, in which the *picayuniversities of America* are depicted as being *full of bumptious little professors who would not be allowed to sweep out a laboratory in London or Berlin.*)

In all the alchemical traditions, as one evokes gods, beseeches archangels and conjures demons, the necessity of exact taxonomy and correct pronunciation can't be overemphasized. Hence, among occultists, the most serious of all the Decalogue's clauses is the fourth, lest the wrath of the entity be brought down.

The invocation of lesser forces (spirit, angel, demon, elemental) is exact, since love doesn't enter into it so much. In one sense it's far more dangerous than the invocation of gods. In the higher work you are actually wooing the god—it is an act of art. In the lower you are compelling—it is an act of science.
—Jack Parsons

Like Jesus having the tassel of his cloak tugged and feeling the healing power go forth from his person unauthorized, no higher being can abide promiscuous buttonholing, and is likely to turn and rebuke, as in the following instance of unwelcome feminine approach from behind:

And a certain woman, which had an issue of blood twelve years, and had suffered many things of many physicians, and had spent all that she had, and was nothing bettered, but rather grew worse, when she had heard of Jesus, came in the press behind, and touched his garment. For she said, If I may touch but his clothes, I shall be whole. And straightway the fountain of her blood was dried up; and she felt in her body that she was healed of that plague. And Jesus, immediately knowing in himself that virtue had gone out of him, turned him about in the press, and said, Who touched my clothes?
—Mark 5:25-30

(Cf. notes 1 and 153 for Christian Rosenkreutz and Cyliani's prepositionally parallel, but qualitatively opposite encounters.)

As far as the present annotator has been able to ascertain, the "young lady," Nabokov's *dwarf Kali*, was never heard from again. She ended up an octogenarian emeritus colleague of Siegfried Tolliot in the Creative Writing department at the abovementioned Nevada community college. She voluntarily shares an infernal faculty meeting table with the priapic eunuch many afternoons per week, deep into the cold desert evening. Her *issue* far from *dried up*, her *plague* yet *unhealed*, she regales her fellow damned over and over again with the tale of the time, toward the middle of the previous century, when she came into contact, briefly, with the garment of genius.

139.   *Better a woman...better a lover...better a body of matter...love again*

Our poet is preparing us for the shock of re-entry, on the Esau's-heel of "Dr. Ripley," into Carnalized Mom's *material body*.

(See note 127.)

140. *snakes entwined in lust…my own unraveling*

For the boa constrictor and caduceus in esoteric Mariolatry, cf. note 105.

141. Not the muscular sculptor and painter of sculptural musculature of whom the coming and going women talk in Prufrock's room. They wouldn't be talking of Fuseli, but tittering and whispering about his grotesque *Midsummer Night's Dream* fairies, lubriciously limned more or less by accident at the improvisatory moment of execution with dry pigment sloshed together with turpentine, linseed oil and gold size.

This identification with Fuseli can only be deliberate misdirection and feint on the part of our monumental poet, supreme technician that he is—unless this is a sincere plea to be *freed* from his high seriousness, as symptomatized by the *unknown words, script* and *tongue* that *pound in his head* like a stone carver's chisels.

142. *Westerlies*

This particular wind, unlike the southerly (see line 17), blows but once in the Bible, as follows:

> *And the Lord turned a mighty strong west wind, which took away the locusts, and cast them into the Red sea; there remained not one locust in all the coasts of Egypt.*
> —Exodus 10:19

The author of Exodus was no stranger to alchemy's finely-sifted particulations, as in this previous-but-one attempt:

And the Lord said unto Moses and unto Aaron, Take to you handfuls of ashes of the furnace, and let Moses sprinkle it toward the heaven in the sight of Pharaoh. And it shall become small dust in all the land of Egypt, and shall be a boil breaking forth with blains upon man, and upon beast, throughout all the land of Egypt. And they took ashes of the furnace, and stood before Pharaoh; and Moses sprinkled it up toward heaven; and it became a boil breaking forth with blains upon man, and upon beast. And the magicians could not stand before Moses because of the boils; for the boil was upon the magicians, and upon all the Egyptians.
—Exodus 9:8-11

Since breezes must have distributed the infectious ash, there is no reason to suppose larger meteorological phenomena would be beyond the horned one's grasp. However, the merciful intent behind the Westerly's deployment is implausible in the giver of laws to our first canto's white phosphorizers.

143. Some of the Linear B texts from Knossos speak of a sanctuary called Daidaleion, within whose no doubt labyrinthine precincts all the gods were propitiated, in particular *qe-ra-si-ja*, otherwise unknown. This entity is also referred to as *qe-ra-si-jo*. As elsewhere in our poem, there is linguistic reason to suspect androgyny, hermaphroditism, or perhaps artificially induced transgenderism:

If the endings -ia[s] and -ios represent an ethnikonic suffix, then this means "The One From Qeras[os]". If aspirated, *Qhera- would have become "Thera-" in later Greek.

> *"Therasia" and its ethnikon "Therasios" are both attested in later Greek; and, since -sos was itself a genitive suffix in the Aegean Sprachbund, *Qeras could also shrink to *Qera. An alternate view takes qe-ra-si-ja and qe-ra-si-jo as proof of androgyny, and applies this name by similar arguments to the legendary seer, Tiresias, but these views are not mutually exclusive of one another. If qe-ra-si-ja was an ethnikon first, then in following him/her/it the Cretans also feared whence it came.*
> —*Minoan Qe-Ra-Si-Ja: The Religious Impact of the Thera Volcano on Minoan Crete*

The Knossan Linear B texts also mention *a-ne-mo I-je-re-ja*, a honey-collecting Priestess of the Winds (*hiereia anemon*), presumably all four and not just the southerly or westerly.

Our poet is making a sing-song invocation of the Cretan Tiresias, perhaps to catch the attention of his sweet breezy priestess, who shares the sanctuary. The summons is successful, as the blush of the following passage makes clear.

144.   *Rubedo* is the alchemical reddening, purpling, or *iosis*. In Jungian terms, this symbolizes Individuation, the self made whole, the poet united and intermingled with his honey.

145.   *deep red, blood red, love red…napkins rinsed time and time again…trace of her lips*

The *blood* is catamenia. The *napkins* are sanitary, and they're *rinsed* of uterine sloughage and unfecundated eggs. The *lip-traces* are left by labia minora. (See passim for menorrhagia in this alchemical-Mariolatrous context.)

146.   *More than kisses…absent speak:* John Donne, "To Sir Henry

147

Wotton"

147. Library scientists and archivists observe a convention of sorting names with the (presumably) Scottish and Irish patronymic prefixes simultaneously. This orthographic license makes available the interpretation of this emphatic two-word line to indicate another form of natal *coercion* (cf. note 11), as follows:

> *...Despair thy charm,*
> *And let the angel whom thou still hast served*
> *Tell thee, Macduff was from his mother's womb*
> *Untimely ripped...*
> —*Macbeth*, Act V, scene 8

To go *beyond* the Caesarian-sectioned Thane of Fife would be to engage in inter-cranial self-impregnation, as our poet has done (see note 13; also cf. note 105 for autoparthenogenesis taken to deoxyribonucleic depths).

148. *ranges beyond Chengdu...never conquered*

This would be the Qionglai mountains, daunting even for one so ambitious as Ghengis Khan, fueled on *mare's milk* (cf. line 512). This range includes the famous Tiantai Mountain, where, during the Southern Song Dynasty, Confucianism, Taoism and Buddhism tangled so aggressively that, uniquely in the history of the Flowery Middle Kingdom, a religious inquisition had to be convened, known among the peasants as The Monks' Court. The chief negotiator was significantly not a politician or priest, but a poet, Lu You, who wrote eleven thousand poems, including a couple of forlorn love lyrics that were turned into an opera. He was love's alchemical emissary to China, hence his evocation here, to introduce the next line's *Spirit talk*.

149.   *Spirit talk...qe-ra-si-jo*

Our poet's conjuration of the Knossan Hermaphrodite is repeated, and with repetition takes on an even more sing-song
tone. Cf. note 170 for Israel Regardie on barbarous syllables of
invocation.

150.   Reversal of cronification; illusory tensefulness, just as arbitrary
as the points of the compass. Cf. note 165 and ameliorization of
the personified Nigredo.

151.   *someone else's nose?*

Cf. note 27 for Dr. Joseph Simms' method of determining identity through physiognomical mensuration of nares, bridge and
septum.

152.   In a timeless situation, such as, for example, a Panguitch
Community College faculty meeting, Medusa could have gazed
into the burnished brass shield for a good portion of geologic
time, petrifying herself.

Sometimes, at faculty parties, after the Carlo Rossi has been ra-
tioned, Nabokov's *dwarf Kali* breaks out a nylon-stringed folk
guitar and quavers, in the venerable style of Joan Baez—

I'm goin' down
to the River Jordan

just to bathe my
weary soul.

And if I can touch
the hem o' his garment,
oh, Lordy, I believe
it could make me whole.

(Cf. note 171 for Zeena Schreck on the superannuated tantric crone, through whose utter physical repulsiveness the Vama Marga adept can learn to suppress his gag reflex, *à la* Linda Lovelace, but to an ostensibly higher, or at least deeper purpose.)

153. Thus our well-traveled and long-lived *fair and glorious lady*, our *Woman Clothed in the Sun*, took her leave of French alchemist Cyliani. Like Christian Rosenkreutz before him, Cyliani was accosted from behind, but rather less gently, and in less carnalized terms, by an *astral spirit or ardent spirit which* [was] *a projection from the pole star*:

> *I thought that I heard split the tree at whose feet I was sitting. The sound made me turn my head. I saw a nymph, a very epitome of beauty emerging from this tree. Her clothes were so diaphanous that they seemed transparent.*
>
> *She said to me, "…My essence is celestial. You can even consider me as a ray from the pole star. My power is such that I animate everything. I am the astral spirit. I give life to everything that breathes and vegetates. I know everything.*
> —*Hermès Dévoilé*

This "epitome of beauty" appears and withdraws three times in Cyliani's account, as does Christ at the end of Revelation, and Hamlet's father's ghost, who comes and goes twice, and makes it three with a strictly aural manifestation: "Swear," insufflating like Sophia into our poet's ear in Gaza. Triple repetition is requisite in jokes and fairy tales of all times and places..

154. That the knots are not Gordian, but are named for the short-cut solution of the original perplexity, implies that the divorce in the next line is not broached in jest, as the relationship already promises to be short-lived.

155.   *Batter my heart, three-personed God, for you*
    As yet but knock, breathe, shine, and seek to mend;
    That I may rise, and stand, o'erthrow me, and bend
    Your force to break, blow, burn, and make me new.
    I, like an usurped town, to another due,
    Labour to admit you, but Oh, to no end.
    Reason, your viceroy in me, me should defend,
    But is captived, and proves weak or untrue.
    Yet dearly I love you, and would be loved fain,
    But am betrothed unto your enemy:
    Divorce me, untie or break that knot again,
    Take me to you, imprison me, for I,
    Except you enthrall me, never shall be free,
    Nor ever chaste, except you ravish me.
    —John Donne, "Batter my heart, three-person'd God" (Holy Sonnet XIV)

Cf. note 112 for a quasi-apocalyptic vulgarization of the metaphysical conceit of being ravished by a trinity, or *trimurti*.

156. *Florence and Sienna…you can't escape them*

The only two alchemists named in the Inferno are natives of these two inescapable cities. Capocchio and Griffolino d'Arezzo were burnt at the stake and consigned to perdition among the "falsifiers" in the tenth ditch of the Eighth Circle.

> *"And thou shalt see I am Capocchio's shade,*
> *Who metals falsified by alchemy;*
> *Thou must remember, if I well descry thee,*
>
> *How I a skilful ape of nature was..."*
>
> *"I of Arezzo was," one made reply,*
> *"And Albert of Siena had me burned;*
> *But what I died for does not bring me here.*
>
> *'Tis true I said to him, speaking in jest,*
> *That I could rise by flight into the air,*
> *And he who had conceit, but little wit,*
>
> *Would have me show to him the art; and only*
> *Because no Daedalus I made him, made me*
> *Be burned by one who held him as his son.*
>
> *But unto the last Bolgia of the ten,*
> *For alchemy, which in the world I practised,*
> *Minos, who cannot err, has me condemned."*

These alchemists are tormented by the ravenous shades of two other falsifiers—not of metals but identities (the more severe offense in Dante's mind): Gianni Schicchi, who by impersonation was able to join the Florentine *nouveau riche* (much despised by Dante); and Myrrha, who, in Ovid's *Metamorphoses*, by the clever ruse of assuming a false name, was able to use her father just as Siegfried Tolliot, under the alias of Bare-Naked Dinkus Boy, "pulled a Lot's daughter" on Ezra Pound in Saint Elizabeth's Hospital.

If, as several psychoanalytically-inclined critics have suggested, Siegfried Tolliot considered his victim a father figure, and if, in insinuating his residual priapism into the latter's superannuated fundament, he was acting out some convoluted burlesque of an Electra complex, or attempting to relieve something so trite and wrongheaded as Harold Bloom's "anxiety of influence," then the Bare-Naked Dinkus Boy would qualify, no less than the mother of Adonis, for residency in this tenth ditch of the Eighth Circle.

A falsifier may feign to be who he's not, but the city he can never escape is that municipality walled hereditarily within his bosom. Griffolino was not only born but burned in Siena; and Tolliot, as it turns appallingly out, though not dead yet, shows every sign of spiralling down the same redundant cycle:

> *Apart from my moniker tarred with the toothbrush*
> *that fails to abrade sickly plaque from the rictus*
> *of smarmy professors, my shamefullest secret*
> *(I trust you won't spill it) concerns Siegfried's*
> *pitiful lieu de naissance: it's no less grotesquely*
> *than Hailey was Ezra's that Panguitch is mine.*
>
> *The MFA lectern-cum-neighborhood barbecue*
> *make an unchymical auto-da-fé,*
> *and I'm to be roasted like poor Griffolino,*
> *but sans immortality teased out in tercets,*
> *rather by dactyls that skeletomusculaturally grind*
> *Castrato and Bollocks to charcoal briquettes...*
> —excerpt from *Bare-Naked Dinkus Boy Meets Jane Pauley*

To which compare Dante's vision of a similar damnation:

> *I saw two seated, propped against each other,*
> *As pan on pan is propped to keep them hot,*
> *And pocked, each one, from head to foot with scabs.*
>
> *And I have never seen a stableboy*

153

Comb a horse more quickly when his master
Awaits him or he reluctantly stays up

Than I saw these two scratch themselves with nails
Over and over because of the burning rage
Of the fierce itching which nothing could relieve.

The way their nails scraped down upon the scabs
Was like a knife scraping off scales from carp
Or some other sort of fish with larger scales.

"O you there tearing at your mail of scabs
And even turning your fingers into pincers..."
—*Inferno*, lines 70-85

Tolliot's reply:

As Dante's Gehenna resounds with the scratches
of damned dermatitics, just so does the ditch
in which Tolliot itches get stuffed with the bitch
who blasphemed the bald nymphet.
Thus Panguitch is named for the doubled-up insult
of deep-seated aching and skin irritation....
—excerpt from *Bare-Naked Dinkus Boy Meets Jane Pauley*

Sienna: Our poet spells Griffolino's hometown with the double "n" to call attention to the famous local pigment which, in its production, like so many artificial colors of the Medieval and Renaissance periods, engages certain stages of the alchemical process, in this case the final two. It begins with a type of yellow clay, called limonite, representing the penultimate stage of *citrinitas* or *xanthosis*, which in the Jungian program of post-psychoanalytical individuation, stands for the wise codger. Heat is applied, and iron oxide in the limonite turns to red haematite. This is the *rubedo*, the individuated self in Jung's system. The pigment sienna was known and esteemed as *terra rossa* in Dante's time.

157.   *I have been sometimes inclined to think, that the reason*
       why GOD tells Moses, "Thou canst not see My face; for
       there shall no man see Me and live," might be, that, as
       transcendent objects destroy the sense, so lovely and glorious
       a sight (whose continuance shall make our happiness in
       heaven), would let in joys, and would create desires, too
       mighty for frail mortality to sustain. The ravished soul,
       being shown such a game, would break the leashes that
       tie her to the body, and thereby hinder her flight to that
       wished union; and the glad heart, to narrow a receptacle
       for so much joy, to make room for such guests, would stretch
       into a rupture.
       —Robert Boyle, *Some motives to the Love of God*

Like Griffolino, Robert Boyle claimed to offer human flight, a *game that would break the leashes that tie* not the *soul* to the *body*, but the body to the earth. In his case it was mechanically induced, himself only claiming influence by alchemy rather than full initiation into the art itself. Hence his death in bed from paralysis, rather than at the stake from flames.

158.   *Moroccan drums…inside the caverns*

The subterranean percussion and torturous dancing comprise the sort of ritual, timeless and terrifying, that has in all places accompanied the ordaining of men into castrato priesthoods.

Morocco was the operating theater Jan Morris chose for his/her elective surgery. (See note 136.) This was reportedly due to the longstanding tradition in Marrakesh of copying and preserving Mussulmannish medical books, such as the alchemical classic

Kitāb al-Burhān fī asrār ʿilm al-mīzān by al-Jaldakī. The latter tome outlines procedures for emptying scrota in a dizzyingly wide array of variations, including one or two late addenda which demonstrate how to turn testicle sacs inside-out for the improvisation of faux-vaginal sleeves. Clearly, this book is a product of an age prior to the current predominantly fundamentalist phase of Islam.

159. John Donne, Letter to Sir Henry Goodyer

160. *There's a very loud amusement park right in front of my present lodgings.*
      —Nabokov, *Pale Fire*

161. *L'illusion est le premier plaisir.*
      —Voltaire, *"La Pucelle d'Orléans"*

162. *Brahms...Debussy...microbial songs*

Over this formulation Wagner looms like a genitally mutilated Wotan. Our poet is intent on diminishing him to dwarfish dimensions.

Brahms, publicly opposed to that composer in the nineteenth century's most famous musical controversy, privately described himself as an enthusiastic Wagnerian, and took delight in the piano reduction of *Der Ring des Nibelungen*.

Debussy, on the other hand, like all his musical countrymen (except Faure), was theoretically wild for Wagner, yet in practice, with his whole-tone thinking derived from the most un-Aryan gamelan ensembles, wrought much subversion on Germanic chromaticism (embodied in Wagner's true descendant, Schoenberg, the only Jew in this music drama).

Our poet invokes these titanic *singers* only to take evasive action and scurry to Switzerland, land of the yodel and alpenhorn, and thence even deeper into Euterpean *Götterdämmerung*, past instruments that make noise with tin reeds, to the *microbes* that *sing* as they crawl into inner ears and feed on tympani stiff with atrophy.

Vincenz is systematically removing music's consolation to prepare us for imminent descent into a Hell so cacophonous that Satan has vacated and taken the wind with him to discourage sound waves. See lines 683-4.

163.   *every smear...primal ink*

King Solomon evoked and pressed into his personal service no fewer than seventy-two demons. When not servicing his whims, these spirits were kept in a brazen jar whose lid, lock and key consisted of magic sigils. *Ars Goetia*, the opening section of the grimoire *Clavicula Salomonis Regis*, contains the specifications of the seventy-two, including their demonic signatures, which comprise *smears, blotches, dots* and *loosely-wrought lines*, most efficacious when rendered in that most *primal ink*: blood.

164.   The first stage of alchemical transformation is the *Nigredo*, a foul *blackened liquid*, gradually transmuted to solid luminescence. In dreams it can be embodied in a deformed crone with puckered and sometimes supernumerary dugs. (Cf. Ephesian Diana: note 104.)

> *...a black woman with three withered arms and six or seven breasts slid herself sideways in front of me. It was at this point that I went and found Richard and said, "I think we'd better get out of here."*

—Terence McKenna, *Third Lecture on Alchemy*

165. *not quite so empty as we once thought*

Representing dross of heart and sludge of psyche, *Nigredo* is often ameliorated, cleaned up as it were, her horrific revelation sanitized to be more presentable to the waking ego, her insights buried under cosmeticization.

> *Nigredo's black unshaped lubricity*
> *gets socialized, elucidated, bleached*
> *by exegesis, epidermis-deep.*
> *Erased is vene varicose's bruise,*
> *unpuckered the old striae distensae.*
> —We'll See Who Seduces Whom

166. *beginning…yet again*

The *re-reader* is so advised. (See note 1 for Nabokov's promulgation.)

167. A Hell without wind must be one which Satan has vacated—

> *Underneath each came forth two mighty wings,*
> *Such as befitting were so great a bird;*
> *Sails of the sea I never saw so large.*
>
> *No feathers had they, but as of a bat*
> *Their fashion was; and he was waving them,*
> *So that three winds proceeded forth therefrom.*
> —Inferno: Canto XXXIV

If, as the Catechism of the Catholic Church tells us, "The chief punishment of Hell is eternal separation from God," and if even the Inferno's spelunker couldn't imagine a Hell so miserable that Satan would abandon it, the place must be made by man, not God, like the botched project of Victor Frankenstein:

> *...it became a thing such as even Dante could not have conceived....*
> —Mary Wollstonecraft Shelley, *Frankenstein*

Here the stale and stifling atmosphere of Siegfried Tolliot's terminal predicament is brought to mind, a nemesis and symbolic retribution prophesied, among many other things, by Pound in his "pillow-bite-talk."

> *When being used like a woman, the codger, as a language man, liked to yammer rather than yowl—though certain of his recorded performances blur the distinction.*
> —Siegfried Tolliot, private email correspondence with the present annotator

On the strength of his article, "The Root of Pound's Wet Black Bough" (*Kanorado Review of the Collective Humanities*, Volume 3, 1981), Tolliot wound up in "the most despicable of purgatories," exactly as he predicted, with self-effacing frankness, in his "fully fingered epyllion," *Bare-Naked Dinkus Boy Meets Jane Pauley:*

> *...I'll end a professor of English in Panguitch,*
> *get tenure and rot and curl up and waste,*
> *while Bare-Naked Dinkus Boy skims the hot skyline*
> *with electromagnetical anchor-girl Pauley*
> *and ransoms America, me and himself*
> *from death and good taste....*

Panguitch Community College, Nevada, is only a few hundred miles south of Pound's Hailey, Idaho, birthplace, where Tolliot, the Creative Writing Department's "Pound Man Emeritus," takes students on field trip-pilgrimages. (Cf. lines 617-8 for the Dantean insurmountability of one's hometown.) On the way back he stops off to make an appearance at Coeur d'Alene, where he goes among the neo-Nazi intelligentsia and barter economists and is celebrated as an "intimate of our poet."

The foregoing itinerary, if it bears no relation to cartographic reality, serves to reassert the flexibility of spatial prepositions. Cf. line 717 for a demonstration of this metaphysical conceit by no less an authority than John Donne.

The particular ditch of northern Nevada in which Panguitch languishes is notorious for the rigor mortis of its air. Kites are unknown among the citizens with legs even shorter than the stunted stubs that convey the adults so haltingly among the alkaline deposits.

Thus the priapic eunuch ends in the very antipode of our poet's world, from which one can embark on a tour of *goyische* antiquity by no conveyance other than the wind. (See lines 15-25.)

168.   *Weave a circle round him thrice,*
       And close your eyes with holy dread,
       For he on honey-dew hath fed,
       And drunk the milk of Paradise.

(Cf. note 112 for this overworked passage turned to fresh and stunning effect in *Fission Among the Fanatics*.)

169.   *we all want to sing…to the ocean?*

The intensifying pronoun here is to be taken in the broadest imaginable sense: males, females, and occupiers of every other point on the gonadal spectrum, not excluding the sundry Tiresias figures in this poem, including the present annotator. The river *we all* sing to is the alchemists' *fiery androgynous water:*

> *The universe is surrounded by the sphere of the stars. Beyond that sphere is the sphere of* Schamayim, *which is the Divine fiery water, the first outflow of the Word of God, the flaming river pouring from the presence of the Eternal.* Schamayim, *the* fiery androgynous water, *divides. The fire becomes the solar fire and the water becomes the lunar water.* Schamayim *is the universal mercury—sometimes called* Azoth—*the measureless spirit of life. The spiritual fiery original water—Schamayim—comes through Eden (in Hebrew, vapor) and pours itself into four main rivers. This is the river of living water—Azoth* [the fiery mercurial essence] *that flows out from the throne of God and the Lamb. In this Eden* [vaporous essence or mist] *is the spiritual earth* [incomprehensible and intangible], *or the dust* Aphar, *out of which God formed* Adam min Haadamah, *the spiritual body of man, which body must sometime become revealed.*
>
> —Georg von Welling, *Opus mago-cabalisticum*

170. Israel Regardie is eloquent and insistent on the hypo- and hyperlexical efficacy of barbarous syllables of invocation, such as these gems from the Enochian Keys of Dr. John Dee:

> *Eca, zodocare, Iad, goho.*
> *Torzodu odo kikale qaa!*
> *Zodacare od zodameranu!*
> *Zodorje, lape zodiredo,*

> *Noco Mada, das Iadapiel!*
> *Ilas! hoatahe Iaidaisrael!*

Bearing no particular import, nonsense sounds by their very lack of significance draw spirits of nihilism and decay, *to eat from the plates of men.*

If numerous critics are mistaken in hearing Eliot's *fart in a barrel* (see note 27) as the Root Tone of Nature, we might be permitted rather to perceive one of these barbarous syllables. It's significant that the consummation with the goddess Mary-Isabella (*fucking on the sofa*) only occurs after the syllable of evocation has been uttered, with the barrel serving as the resonator so frequently found among the kits of magi.

171.   *clogged arteries... Ur-mother*

Zeena Schreck, the physiological (as opposed to cinematic) spawn of Anton LaVey (who legendarily played a cameo role as paternal Satan in the movie discussed above), is eloquent on this particular embodiment of Our Lady of Roses:

> *"... in some Vama Marga sects, very old women repre-*
> *senting Shakti in her crone aspect are chosen to be one's*
> *sexual initiatrix.... [One] of the reasons for selecting such*
> *a mudra is to force the male adept normally accustomed to*
> *only experiencing desire for smooth, toned, youthful bod-*
> *ies—to sustain the same degree of sexual ecstasy with what*
> *he perceives as an elderly hag with wrinkled skin and sag-*
> *ging breasts. Part of the methodical system of general de-*
> *programming and deconditioning of natural instincts and*
> *preferences that all left-hand path adepts must undergo,*
> *such experiences also deepen the initiate's understanding of*
> *the transitory nature of maya and its effect on the senses.*
> *—Demons of the Flesh,* Creation Books (2002)

172.   *Licence my roving hands, and let them go*
       Before, behind, between, above, below. [Emphasis added.]
       O, my America, my Newfoundland....
       —John Donne, Elegy XX, "To His Mistress Going to Bed"

Donne's licentious hands are toying with *prepositions of space*, for the flexibility of which the re-reader is advised to revert to our subtitle and first line, also to Saint Peter's dying apocryphal words. (See note 30.)

No stranger to alchemy (cf. "The Sun Rising," "A Nocturnal upon St. Lucy's Day, being the shortest day," etc.), nor to other arcane pursuits which promise or entail adepthood, Donne is clearly engaging in foreplay with the Elizabethan equivalent of an octo- if not nonogenarian Shakti crone. His America would be the Appalachians, oldest mountain range on this particular planet, where the inhabitants, in their isolation, to this day speak an otherwise long-extinct relic of Donne's own English. He would have been familiar with the contemporary maps of *Apalchen*, published by Diego Gutierrez and Jacques le Moyne de Morgues.

173.   In Appalachian jug bands, the favorite percussion instruments for marking time, or *measuring out the life* of a tune, are the doubled spoons, clattered against dungareed thighs or washboarded across menial labor-callused fingers. If these uncouth utensils can't be said to produce the Root Tone, they do doubly *thunder* like the *forked tongue* that announces our next canto.

174.   *Faithful are the wounds of a friend; but the kisses of an enemy are deceitful.*
       —Proverbs 27:6 (modified and cited by Nostradamus)

175. *a child of…mind*

Cf. line 17, along with accompanying critical apparatus, for the theme of cranial fecundation via auditory meatus as it pertains not only to immaculate virgins like Athena, but to *This Wasted Land* itself, Marc Vincenz's skull-baby, transsexually parented by the Southerly.

176. More examples of Israel Regardie's barbarous syllables of invocation.

177. This is the mechanical cry of the Schwarzwald's doubly degenerate Nibelungen. (Cf. note 63.) They are mooted here as shock-contrast to the Anakim, giants at immemorial odds with the original Levantine Nibelungen. (See below.)

178. *O menstrual blood of the sordid whore*

This is a line from Newton's posthumously discovered alchemical manuscripts. (See note 21.) The metalline form of antimony is "menstrual blood" derived from the raw ore, the "sordid whore."

The whorish aspect derives from antimony's trisulphide, kohl in particular, used as a cosmetic in antiquity. The first verse of the eighth chapter of *The Book of Enoch* points out that the beautification of eyelids and other parts of the face was taught to womankind by the fallen angels. Zosimos heard from no less a personage than Isis the Prophetess that such transmutative lore was given in exchange for sex.

179. Cerberus the hell-hound usually has three heads, but, as with the Fates, one has been added, in a subtle recapitulation of Annotator as nemesis. (See note 23.) Below, the same arithmetic process is applied to the canonical archangels.

180. *gondalieri…coppery manes*

Frightening figures are conjured here, Charons with copper pinched not between their fingers, but extruded through their follicles:

> *The magnetism of a red-haired man, we have found, in almost every nation, is instinctively dreaded. We might quote proverbs from the Russian, Persian, Georgian, Hindustani, French, Turkish, and even German, to show that treachery and other vices are popularly supposed to accompany the rufous complexion. When a man stands exposed to the sun, the magnetism of that luminary causes his emanations to be projected toward the shadow, and the increased molecular action develops more electricity. Hence, an individual to whom he is antipathetic—though neither might be sensible of the fact—would act prudently in not passing through the shadow.*
> —Madame Blavatsky, *Isis Unveiled*, volume II, chapter XII, part I

181. The Nephilim are giants gotten by fallen angels on the daughters of men. *The Book of Enoch* shows the dire comeuppance such miscegenation brings:

> *Then Uriel* (see note 204) *said, Here the angels, who co-*

habited with women, appointed their leaders;

And being numerous in appearance made men profane, and caused them to err; so that they sacrificed to devils as to gods.

For in the great day there shall be a judgment, with which they shall be judged, until they are consumed; and their wives also shall be judged, who led astray the angels of heaven that they might salute them...

Again the Lord said to Raphael, Bind Azazyel hand and foot; cast him into darkness; and opening the desert which is in Dudael, cast him in there.

Throw upon him hurled and pointed stones, covering him with darkness;

There shall he remain for ever; cover his face, that he may not see the light.

The Nephilim were identified with dead Philistine soldiers in a display of the idle punsterism endemic to certain scholarly circles, the very inventors and past masters of *licentious free-association* and *bogus scholarship.* Given enough facile rabbinical tinkering, the Masoretic text of Ezekiel 32:27, *gibborim nophelim:* גִבּוֹרִים נֹפְלִים "mighty that are fallen," can yield *gibborim nephilim:*

And they shall not lie with the mighty that are fallen of the uncircumcised, which are gone down to hell with their weapons of war: and they have laid their swords under their heads, but their iniquities shall be upon their bones, though they were the terror of the mighty in the land of the living.

In his final lines, our poet takes his leave by directing his *re-readers* back to Gaza and Canto One, where time's untensefulness began to be established, and prepositions of space were rendered malleable as white-phosphorized Philistine femurs.

182.   *I am Apep, O thou slain One.*
       Thou shalt slay thyself upon mine altar:
       I will have thy blood to drink.
       For I am a mighty vampire,
       and my children shall suck up the wine of the earth which is blood.
       —Aleister Crowley, *Liber Stellae Rubae sub figura LXVI*, 48-49

Along with the evocation of Choronzon in the Algerian Sahara, this is another of The Great Beast 666's secret lower-digestive sex-magickal rites unconsciously reenacted by Tolliot and Pound at Saint Elizabeth's Mental Hospital.

183.   *One August afternoon, when I was in his hayfield helping*
       him with his man to rake up his hay, I well remember
       his pleading, almost reproachful looks at the sky, when the
       thunder-gust was coming up to spoil his hay. He raked
       very fast, then looked at the cloud, and said, "We are in
       the Lord's hand; mind your rake, George! We are in the
       Lord's hand;" and seemed to say, "You know me; this field
       is mine,—Dr. Ripley's,—thine own servant!
       —Emerson

In our poem's greater context, Emerson's "Dr. Ripley" is to be identified with the great British alchemist of that name, author of *The Compound of Alchymy; or, the Twelve Gates leading to the Discovery of the Philosopher's Stone (Liber Duodecim Portarum)*, dedicated to a very pleased King Edward IV.

Of far greater significance to our purposes, Ripley also wrote *Cantilena Riplaei*, a poem even more "chymical" than *This Wasted Land*. The protagonist is a sterile king (cf. note 44, *I have borne the cup of gonads*) who, in order to regain his gametes, must undertake an especially drastic *katabasic nekyia*: he is compelled to burrow back into, or *reverse-spelunk* his carnalized mother's womb. (Cf. lines 510-15 for our poet's engagement of his own maternal propinquity.)

The title of "Ripley's Song" is straightforward as its subject matter, getting right to the incestuously Sophoclean point that's been pussy-footed around by all our preceding prophets-seers-revelators. Finally, at the end of *This Wasted Land*, the *fair and glorious ladies*, the *pole-star nymphs*, the *Erythraean sybils*, the *Blessed Virgins* and the *rock-a-bye-baby mothers* are permitted to strip-tease away pretense and become frank Jocasta. The riches she offers are not transmuted gold, but the family jewels—and not the kind any Nibelung can schlep to Antwerp. The mystery into which our poet is being initiated turns out to be one of *re-masculation:* the opposite of several others we've encountered on these pages.

184. *Der Wille zur Macht...kiltless Scotsman*

It's not Nietzsche's fault if the highlanders in our poem must go about debased and humiliated, their bare blond bollocks exposed to the darkening sun:

In the Latin malus *(bad)—which I place side by side with the Greek* melas *(black, dark)—the vulgar man can be distinguished as the dark-coloured, and above all as the black-haired* ("hic niger est"), *as the pre-Aryan inhabitants of the Italian soil, whose complexion formed the clearest feature of distinction from the dominant blondes, namely, the Aryan conquering race:—at any rate Gaelic has afforded me the exact analogue* —Fin *(for instance, in the name* Fin-Gal*), the distinctive word of the nobility, finally—good, noble, clean, but originally the blonde-haired man in contrast to the dark black-haired aboriginals.*

The Celts, if I may make a parenthetic statement, were throughout a blonde race; and it is wrong to connect, as Virchow still connects, those traces of an essentially dark--haired population which are to be seen on the more elaborate ethnographical maps of Germany with any Celtic ancestry or with any admixture of Celtic blood: in this context it is rather the pre-Aryan population of Germany which surges up to these districts. (The same is true substantially of the whole of Europe: in point of fact, the subject race has finally again obtained the upper hand, in complexion and the shortness of the skull, and perhaps in the intellectual and social qualities. Who can guarantee that modern democracy, still more modern anarchy, and indeed that tendency to the "Commune," the most primitive form of society, which is now common to all the Socialists in Europe, does not in its real essence signify a monstrous reversion—and that the conquering and master race—the Aryan race, is not also becoming inferior physiologically?)
—On the Genealogy of Morals

185.   *This is no Firth of Forth…King Atra-Hasis*

This king is the eponymous protagonist of an Akkadian poem containing a flood narrative that was castigated and recast for the Gilgamesh epic. The waters he had to navigate in his reed and bitumen boat were *the mother of all.*

186.   Cf. note 183 for another figuration of the un-fingered king.

187.   *seething sea of fingers*

This could be construed as a poetic image for the boundless marsh of reeds that faced the Akkadian Noah. However, no better description exists of Siegfried Tolliot's poetry ("throbbing dactyls"). And, of course, it comes from the greatest critical mind among the modernists.

Cf. note 4 for Pound's diametrically opposite reaction to Mina Loy's poetry. Inspired to rhapsodic syllables of invocation, he coined and conjured the word *logopoeia* to convey her "dance of the intelligence among words and ideas."

The irony, of course, is that, even as she was being apotheosized into the modernist equivalent of the Blessed Virgin, Mina Loy was more conscious than most organisms of her own *matter-miredness* (see note 20). She was trying, through her Christian Science and strange eugenic ambiguity about the "cosmopolitan Jew," to refine herself out of existence, like the eponymous artist portrayed in Joyce's immature novel. Not altogether unconsciously, Mina Loy aspired to the condition of one of the feminine entities who bless and/or curse our poem's numerous alchemists, eunuchs, seers, madmen and poets.

188.   The Anunnaki comprise a certain bureau of gods of Sumer, Akkad, Assyria, and Babylonia. The Torah identifies them with the gigantic Anakim of Canaan, ancestors of the Philistine oaf, Goliath.

> *And they brought up an evil report of the land which they had searched unto the children of Israel, saying, The land, through which we have gone to search it, is a land that eateth up the inhabitants thereof; and all the people that*

we saw in it are men of a great stature. And there we saw the giants, the sons of Anak [i.e., the Nephilim, cf. line 755], which come of the giants: and we were in our own sight as grasshoppers, and so we were in their sight.
—Numbers 13:32-33

189.   *O dearest Levant…for fear to know*

Here we perhaps get a hint of why our poet has chosen to fly over that zone in his previous itineraries, paradisiacal and infernal. (Cf. notes 15 and 117, respectively.)

190.   *quoth the crow, quoth the raven*

In Poe, the latter portentous bird is merely that: foreboding in strict terms of tenseful time. Meanwhile, the superior wisdom of the trans-Khyber sees beneath the former's black feathers an agent of causation's utter discombobulation, as in this brilliant retelling of the ancient Jataka Tale:

Two crows are perched over the city gate, through which a learned Brahman is about to pass. The first crow says, "I'm going to shit on this guy's head."

And the second crow gasps, in horror, "But that's a learned Brahman! He's got all the sacred books memorized. He's got more power than the sun, right at his fingertips. The might of Shiva, Destroyer of Worlds, is a gnat-fart compared to what this prick can do. With a single thought he can cause our whole black-feathered tribe to disappear forever!"

To which the first crow replies, "But I must."

Argument over. Barely giving his friend time to fly away and hide in a cave, the prankster takes aim and pinches off a big one.

While it's still in mid-air, we cut to a different scene across town (a cinematic effect in a tale at least three thousand years old).

A sluggish slave girl has been charged with guarding the municipal pile of cereal as it dries in the sun. She wants to doze off, but whenever she closes her eyes, a little goat sneaks up and steals mouthfuls. So she arms herself with a torch. The next time the goat shows its face, she whacks it and sets its shaggy coat on fire.

It scampers to the royal elephant stable and rolls around in the manger to douse the flames, which spread to the walls and burn the place down, nearly killing a hundred thoroughbred elephants.

The king runs into the streets, distraught, weeping, desperate for expert advice. He sees a learned Brahman, who seems to be scraping something off his head.

"Oh, learned Brahman," cries the king, "with infinite wisdom, with the scriptures committed to memory! What magical medicine can you recommend for my hundred elephants, each one of whom I love as my own child? I have manpower at my disposal. If need be, I will levy every able-bodied subject in my kingdom to scour the countryside for whatever ingredients you deem necessary. We must prepare a poultice, recondite and potent, that will soothe the vast, broiled hides of my beloved elephants. What do you prescribe?"

"Crow fat," mutters the Brahman. "Barrels and barrels of fresh crow fat."
—"A Jataka Tale Retold," *Hemorrhaging Slave of an Obese Eunuch* (Dog Horn Books)

191. Ambiguation of the Manfred Mann song, "Doo Wah Diddy Diddy," 1964.

Manfred Mann was born Manfred Sepse Lubowitz, October, 1940, in Johannesburg, Transvaal, Union of South Africa. He is descended from Jewish *uitlanders* ("foreigners") who assimilated among white Afrikaans-speakers and were labeled *Boerejode* (Boer Jews).

It's not known whether Lubowitz's ancestors took part in the Great Trek of the 1830-40's, in which Boers vacated the British Cape Colony and established several of their own republics to the north, to sidestep anti-slavery laws, and to avoid the constant attacks by savage native Xhosas.

Among these Xhosas are female diviners called Amagqirha. They specialize in prophesying via a trance state that involves barbarous syllables of invocation, an addled gait and gyration of the hands. This trance is vividly depicted in one of Lubowitz's most successful recordings. The lyrics were written by Americans Jeff Barry and Elie Greenwich, who knew nothing of the Amaggirha, but it is widely supposed that Lubowitz believes the words came in dreams via transoceanic revelation from the ghosts of the Xhosa diviners killed by British colonists:

There she was just a-walkin' down the street,
singin' "Do wah diddy diddy dum diddy do,"
Snappin' her fingers and shufflin' her feet,
singin' "Do wah diddy diddy dum diddy do."

See passim for numerous instances of revelations, apparitions and internal locutions from female spirits and seeresses.

192. John Donne has completed his metaphysical grope of the Appalachians' superannuated breasts and buttocks (see lines 715-717), and has commenced his post-coital katabasis to parts where *Virginia becomes flat*: the neighborhood where, according to his drinking companion, William Strachey—

> [The Powhatan Indians] *miserably slaughtered...men, women, and children of the first plantation at Roanoak ...(who 20. and od yeeres had peacably lyved and intermixed with thos Savadges, and were out of his Territory).*

This behavior would lend credence to later theories that certain Amerinds were descended from lost tribes of Canaan's genocidal conquerors. And yet, native American cosmology and anthropology displayed a far greater sophistication than the Jews'. Strachey's colleague, Thomas Harriot, a charter member of Sir Walter Raleigh's School of Atheism, had discussed such subjects with the Powhatans, and brought their wisdom home to London, to enflame the blasphemous pre-Adamitism of Christopher Marlowe:

> *That the Indians, and many authors of antiquity, have assuredly written of above 16 thousand years agone, whereas Adam is proved to have lived within six thousand years....* [Marlowe] *affirmeth that Moses was but a juggler, and that one* [Thomas] *Hariot* [sic] *being Sir Walter Raleigh's man can do more than he.*
> —Richard Baines' note to Queen Elizabeth's Privy Council

Donne, as a cleric, surely bowed out of the banter when such a subject was broached at the Mermaid Tavern:

Whoere thou bee that reade this sullen Writt,
Which just so much courts thee, as thou do'st it,
Let me arrest thy thoughts; wonder with mee
Why plowing, building, rulinge and the rest,
And most of those arts, whence our lives are blest,
By cursed Cain's race invented bee,
And blest Seath vext us with Astronomy.
There's nothing simply good or ill alone,
Of every qualitie comparison
The only measure is, and judge, Opinion.
—*The Progress of the Soul*

PRE-ADAMITE, n. One of an experimental and apparently unsatisfactory race of antedated Creation and lived under conditions not easily conceived. Melsius believed them to have inhabited "the Void" and to have been something intermediate between fishes and birds. Little its known of them beyond the fact that they supplied Cain with a wife and theologians with a controversy.
—Ambrose Bierce, *Devil's Dictionary*

193. *In the crud of my discovery…you damn know-it-all…frighteningly cold*

Nearing the end of his labors, our poet has a moment of fatigue and snaps at his dutiful annotator, accusing the latter of intellectual exhibitionism, of taking the *crud of his discovery* and "encircling" (subtending) *This Wasted Land* with questionable sorts of characters: alchemists and dead mythological monarchs.

Immediately after venting unkindness upon his hard-working assistant's head, our poet goes on a vacation, as if to apologize by acknowledging his need for leisure's recruitment. He heads straight for the extreme (as opposed to middling) orient.

194.   *Marco Il Milione…city of heaven…live and die*

This is Hangzhou, marveled at by Marco Polo. Its paradisiacal West Lake was graced by the presence of the Southern Song Dynasty poets here catalogued. (See note 148 for Lu Lou's adjudication of China's only religious inquisition.)

Ironically, if our poet intended, as on his two previous flights, to avoid Palestine and its occupiers, he winds up in the very city where the rare Chinese Jews congregated, built their synagogue and shunned pork before gravitating to Kaifeng.

Matteo Ricci was the first European to register their exotic existence. He showed them an image of the Madonna and Child, whom they took, logically, for Rebecca with one of her twins. They assumed the infant, depicted with a ruddy European complexion rather than Mongolian yellow, must not be Jacob, but rather his slightly older brother, still proverbially red from his birth trauma, as per Genesis 25:25. (Cf. note 89 for this other brace of brothers.) The Chinese Jews imagined the lad eventually selling his birth right not for a mess of red lentil pottage, but a bowl of fermented yeast rice (紅麴米), which in their land is turned an Esau color by cultivation with the mold *Monascus purpureus*. Their copy of the Pentateuch was too old to have the diacritics that might have clarified the menu. (Cf. note 120 on the Masoretic rabbis.)

195. *ate the paper…all that water…time's end*

Some of the Hangzhou Hebrews went to Beijing and got initiated into papistry by Jesuits. With *all that* (baptismal) *water* they
returned back to time's end (John's Apocalypse), where, perhaps
not in complete consciousness, they put themselves in a spiritual
position to *eat paper*, as follows:

*Either spirit exists or it's a phantasm—or maybe it con-
stitutes some mentally masturbatory Heisenberg quibble
that doesn't exist but nevertheless obtains. In any case, the
most intimate access we have to the collective soul's un-
generated immateriality comes in, and on, books. In this
postlapsarian shit-hole of an earth, the naked spirit is presented as nearly unencumbered with existence as it can be
via a thin layer of inky molecules on paper. A book is the
closest the insensible can come to being sensed, as John of
Patmos knew. In his insular malnourishment he made a
bagel sandwich of it:*

*And I saw a mighty angel come down from heaven, clothed
with a cloud: and a rainbow was upon his head, and his
face was as it were the sun, and his feet as pillars of fire.
And he had in his hand a little book open…And he said
unto me, Take the little book, and* eat it up. [Emphasis
added.]
—Revelation 10:1-2, 9

*Writing, if good, transcends time as handily as space, and
constitutes the only human permanence. We have no idea
what the kithara sounded like before or after Milesian
Timotheus added a string to it. Apelles' paintings are lost
tantalizations. Meanwhile, Plato's dialogues are realer,
more present, than the dork in the next cubicle.*
—*Put It Down in a Book* (Drill Press)

The Chinese Jews' conversion experience was uncannily recapitulated, in cruel burlesque, by their later coreligionists. Sent by Mao to Qinghai death camp on charges of pandering to feudal superstition, they served as guinea pigs for experiments in human nutrition that included the fatal forced consumption of that peculiarly Chinese invention, in literal sheets and rolls rather than bound in metaphorical "little books."

196. *where the toilet is a road…Siegfried…Herodotus*

Tolliot is here presented as a witness of Panguitch's squalor *(plastic bags are free-roaming)*. The implication is that he's every bit as reliable on extreme northern Nevada as Herodotus was on the Middle East—though the latter never mentions Solomon's Temple nor the ostensible people who would have worshipped in it.

197. *These, which your highness here doth see, Are leaves of Hermes' secret tree.*
    —from a manuscript in the Bodleian Library, Ashmole 1421.

The Tree of Hermes is an alchemical key condensed into a list fourteen points by Samuel Norton, great-grandson of Thomas Norton (c.1433-c.1513), author of the *Ordinall of Alchemy*. The fourteen points are as follows:

1. Solution, the act of passing a gaseous or solid condition into one of liquidity.
2. Filtration, the mechanical separation of a liquid from the undissolved particles suspended in it.
3. Evaporation, the changing or converting from a liquid or solid state into a vaporous state with the aid of heat.
4. Distillation, an operation by which a volatile liquid

may be separated from substances which it holds in solution.

5. Separation, the operation of disuniting or decomposing substances.

6. Rectification, the process of refining or purifying any substance by repeated distillation.

7. Calcination, the conversion into a powder or calx by the action of heat; expulsion of the volatile substance from a matter.

8. Commixtion, the blending of different ingredients into one compound or mass.

9. Purification (through putrefaction), disintegration by spontaneous decomposition; decay by artificial means.

10. Inhibition, the process of holding back or restraining.

11. Permentation, the conversion of organic substances into new compounds in the presence of a ferment.

12. Fixation, the act or process of ceasing to be a fluid and becoming firm; state o being fixed.

13. Multiplication, the act or process of multiplying or increasing in number, the state of being multiplied.

14. Projection, the process of transmuting the base metals into gold.

A dutiful and doctrinaire Jungian with the proper medical degrees can presumably sublimate each clause in this quattuordecalogue, in all its particulars, to the process of Individuation.

Siegfried Tolliot, with no formal training in the field, has claimed in private email correspondence to have passed in perfect consciousness through each of these twice-seven points on his way to blossoming as Bare Naked Dinkus Boy. This light-speed transformation supposedly took place, one point per day, during the two weeks after his testicles were excised in 1958.

Apparently, in accordance with Samuel Norton's first step *(Solu-*

tion…*passing a solid condition into a state of liquidity)*, the loose pair of items were placed in a blender. Four years old at the time, by a synchronicity Tolliot can't help but tout as "supremely Jungian," the minor kitchen appliance in deployment happened to have been the millionth price unit vended by the Waring corporation.

From there, his pureed parts are supposed to have gone through *separation from undissolved particles, disuniting, discomposing, conversion into a calx, putrefaction by artificial means, ferment, fixation, multiplication,* and so on and so forth, etc., straight up the fourteen-branched trunk of the Hermetical Tree, until, finally, the desiderated *projection* was achieved. This, we are asked to believe, coincided with Tolliot's modernist adventure in the "schizy ward" of Saint Elizabeth's mental hospital.

The result was a couple of literal nuggets, suitable for mounting as cufflinks, to be worn to faculty Christmas parties at Panguitch Community College and kept in a little chamois bag the rest of the year, as protection from the alkaline northern Nevada air.

This narrative contradicts Tolliot's own *Castrato and Ballock*s trope, by which he depicts himself toting the former contents of his scrotum, fetish-wise, untransmuted, preserved in salt, much like Japanese salarymen's jerked and boxed umbilical cords. (See note 44.) Thus the priapic eunuch exposes his own compulsive mendacity, even as it distorts the most intimate details of his physiology. For more barely sublimated psychosexual lies, cf. *Afterword.*

198.   *Who is that really on the other side of you?*

Cf. line 75 for this question in *The Waste Land*; and see note 29 for the answer in *This Wasted Land*.

199. This is Giordano Bruno's answer to the question, "Why is love symbolized by fire?" in *The Heroic Frenzies*, which he wrote while spying on papists in London's French embassy for Queen Elizabeth.

Bruno's satirical writings and sardonic personality rendered him unemployable in Marburg and Prague, and caused his dismissal from lectureships in Wittenburg and Helmstedt. He finally secured a job tutoring a patrician who found Bruno so personally objectionable that he denounced him to the inquisition and got him burned at the stake. In this career path, Bruno resembles an earlier satirist:

We don't know what Juvenal said to [imperial favorite] *Paris, but it must have been as savagely indignant as his poetry, because it got him smacked from Italy, from Europe, clear out of the ballpark known today as the temperate zone. While circumspect Martial was allowed to stick around and take pleasure cruises down to Naples, to be seen affecting Grecian attire and angling for sardines off the porticoes of rich patrons' bayside vacation villas, our impolitic Juvenal was exiled among the beast-worshipping fellaheen of Upper Egypt, from which inhospitable outpost even the hardiest centurion returned prematurely decrepit, if at all. He was damned to Syene, the driest city in the world, previously known to the prophet Ezekiel as Seveneh, the absolute southernmost limit of Egypt, after which came the no-man's land of Ethiopia. The natives so far upriver were not habitual cannibals—just when they got drunk. Talk about a hardship post. It was definitely not Alexandria with its generous colonnades and cool marble porticoes. The coiners of the famous phrase "Bum-Fuck Egypt" surely had Juvenal's place of banishment in mind.*

> Broiling there on the cancerous tropic, Syene was the sec-
> ond grimmest frontier outpost known in those days be-
> fore the unfortunate discovery of Japan (where I languish
> now).
> —*Fission Among the Fanatics* (Spuyten Duyvil Books)

(Cf. note 167 for the inhospitality of Tolliot's place of terminal
banishment.)

200. *"More, More!"*

By contrast, the birds in Nostradamus' Epistle to Henry II cry
"Now, Now!" (See note 47.) A coital connection is formed with
the *ejaculatio praecox* of Christ's *I come quickly* in the last chapter
of Revelation, and the *-postcox* of Vincenz's *HURRY UP PLEASE
ITS TIME* at the premature "close" of our poem in a previous
canto. (See lines 400-19.) Nostradamus' birds appeared in the
middle of *This Wasted Land*, vocalizing as if in the moment of
orgasm. The present seagulls, here at the actual end, are gasping
for a resumption of coitus. This is re-reading taken to the pelvic
level.

201. *singed flesh…Moorish shashlik*

Even in the polymathic ecstasy of his closing lines, our poet
won't deprive us of his exquisite gastronmization.

202. *Ma il passione e morte…our third vanishes into dark flooded corners*

To get himself and his insufflating Sophia a little privacy, our
poet makes an understandable but fruitless attempt to dispense
with the present annotator once and for all by drowning him/
her in labyrinthine darkness. (Cf. lines 75 and 842 for *the feckless*

third.)

Vincenz announces his awareness that murdering such a faithful, blameless and humble servant smacks of the *passione e morte* of Christ. But even such a deliberate sacrifice will take no more effect on our text than the cruel rebuke previously unloaded on the present annotator's head. (See line 801.) End notes, by definition, come and remain after the primary text has achieved its fulness. A poem printed on anything less than a Möbius strip, no matter how many exhortations it makes to *re-readers*, is scheduled for the eventual full stop.

Cf. note 23 for the figure of Annotator as Nemesis.

203. A particularly exquisite example of our poet's concise phrases that writhe with multiple ironies. Malthusian life-boat ethics with their fatalistic spiral into death are, by their very nature, no more *cyclical* than they are liable to be *invigorated*.

204. At this late point, our poet must have in mind one purana in particular:

> *The end of everything is going to be like a jumbo jet crash: what kills you is the sheer bouncing avoirdupois of all the other assholes jam-packed around you. The unprecedented apocalyptic monstrosity of the internet makes it obvious that our universe, and everybody in it, is hurtling into the final few screams of the Great Dissolution, as promised in the Vishnu Purana. The Night of Brahma will follow, when we all have to shut the fuck up, and even stop publishing e-books.*
> —author's foreword to the electronic edition of *My Hands Were Clean* (Unlikely Books)

205. Speaking here is an Enochian entity with *The knowledg of Metalls*. Prince BORNOGO is resplendent in a red robe, with a *Gold Cerclet on his hed* (the same outfit worn by Madame Blavatsky in her London soirees). He materializes in John Dee's *De Heptarchia Mystica (Diuinis, Ipsius Creationis, Stabilis Legibus)*, or On the Mystical Rule of the Seven Planets, a grimoire—or (euphemistically) a method book for summoning angels.

The prince holds forth as follows:

> *I am BORNOGO. This is my Seale. This my true Char-acter. What thow desyrest in me, shal be fullfilled. Glory to God....Behold, Behold, lo Behold my mighty powre con-sisteth in this. Lerne wisdome by my words. This is wrowght for thy erudition what I entrust thee from God. Loke unto thy Chardg truely: Thow art yet dead. Thow shalt be revyved. But oh blesse God truely. The blessing, that God giueth me: I will bestow uppon thee, by omission. O how mighty is our God: which walked on the waters: which sealed me with his name: whose Glory is withoute ende. Thow hast written me, but yet dost not know me. Use me in the Name of God: I shall at the tyme appointed be ready. I will Manifest the works of the Seas: And the Miracles of the depe, shall be known.*
> —Chapter II

Dr. Dee brings forth this august entity, and many others, with the assistance of the archangel Uriel, who presides over chaos and terror. In *The Book of Enoch*, Uriel helps Raphael bring comeup-pance on Azazyel, leader of the fallen angels who fathered un-couth giants on the daughters of men. (See note 181.)

The canonical archangels are Gabriel (a.k.a. the Holy Ghost's pimp: see note 13), Michael and Raphael. (The latter appears in the *Book of Tobit*, in the Catholic and Orthodox bibles.) When a fourth is needed to make up the cardinal points of the compass, Uriel is pressed into service by the Christian Gnostics, by Pope "Not Angles but Angels" Gregory I, and in the pseudo-Dionysian *De Coelesti Hierarchia*.

The same pattern is followed above, when our poet finds it expedient to add a Fate (see note 23) and to supply the hell-hound with an extra head (see line 753).

> *Thither came Uriel, gliding through the even*
> *On a sun-beam, swift as a shooting star*
> *In autumn thwarts the night, when vapours fired*
> *Impress the air, and shows the mariner*
> *From what point of his compass to beware*
> *Impetuous winds....*
> —Milton, *Paradise Lost*

206. Joseph Mede, possibly Milton's teacher at Christ's College, in the "Fourth Phial" of his *Clavis Apocalyptica (On the Sun of the Bestial Heaven)*, writes as follows:

> *That we may discover what the sun is in the world of the beast, we must first see what the heaven is in that world, lest otherwise, destitute of the clew of analogy, we wander too much from the mark. For the sun is not to be placed, or conceived to exist, but in a heaven suitable to it. The heaven, then, of the antichristian world is the supreme and universal pontifical power itself, or, in short, whatever exists of more sublime and regal authority in any part of the bestial world; that is, in the whole community of provinces acknowledging the Roman pontiff as their head. For so, in the natural world, all that is on high, and above the*

earth and waters, is called heaven, in the acceptation of the Hebrews, and of the Holy Spirit.... Now on this sun is the fourth phial forthwith to be poured out; so that he, driven out of his usual course in the heaven of the beast, and shining in a different manner, may scorch and torment with heat and fervour, even to blasphemy, the inhabitants of the antichristian world, whom he was formerly accustomed greatly to cheer with his warmth and radiance.

207.   *Sweet Wizard, in whose footsteps I have trod*
        Unto the shrine of the most obscene god,
        So steep the pathway is, I may not know,
        Until I reach the summit where I go.
       —Victor Benjamin Neuburg, *The Triumph of Pan*

These lines were addressed to Aleister Crowley, under whose magickal sway Neuburg assisted in the evocation of the horrendous Choronzon, Keeper of the Threshold. The prelude to that working, along with the personal idiosyncrasies of Neuburg himself, have been fictionally realized with near supernatural vividity in *Elmer Crowley: a katabasic nekiya* (Mandrake of Oxford Press):

The potency inherent in blood, daubed and pooled with correct ceremoniousness at each point of a Triangle of Art, can furnish immaterial beings the stuff to make themselves manifest, obnoxious, horrifying and dangerous. Few in my considerable experience manifested more offputtingly than Brother I-Will-Conquer-All [a.k.a. Victor Neuburg] *after I tarted him up in the Sahara. And I didn't need to draw or shed a single daub of blood, as he was already a very material being—though he wound up doubting that with all his ruined mind.*

The makeover was necessary to offset the bewitching effect of his pretty Hebrew buttocks. Just two daubs of deep red dye did the trick, applied to a couple tufts of his head hair, Afro-Asiatically kinky, which were pulled up and tied to resemble devil horns.

I led the conquering brother around by a choke chain. To the native way of seeing, he could be nothing other than a djinn lured and captured with the usual hemorrhage splotches in the sand. This clever ruse served to frighten off the few Bedouins and Berbers we didn't feel like sodomizing at the moment, who might otherwise distract us from the serious work we'd come to do.

It's not as though the costume did all the work of putting the savages off. Plenty of people's peculiarities become exaggerated abroad in sultry latitudes, out from under society's microscope. But even back in London and without my ministrations, Brother I-Will-Conquer-All wasn't the most presentable young man on the street. He washed just about as often as the average djinn, and dressed the lower half of his body with even less frequency. He never spoke unless spoken to, then spasmed and convulsed appallingly, so that whatever words came out were unintelligible. His laugh was indescribable, the cruelest caricature of an Israelitish cackle—cloaking, of course, a moroseness equal to that displayed by his Mishnaic coreligonists, who mitose and parturate against their will. [Cf. note 11.] Brother I-Will-Conquer-All's guffaws of agony and shrieks of hilarity needed, as they say, to be heard to be believed.

Crowley's appraisal of Neuburg on the page was decidedly different:

...he produced some of the finest poetry of which the En-

*glish language can boast. He had an extraordinary deli-
cacy of rhythm, an unrivalled sense of perception, a purity
and intensity of passion second to none, and a remarkable
command of the English language.*
—Aleister Crowley, *Autohagiography*

Ezra Pound delivered a far less charitable appraisal of Siegfried
Tolliot's "throbbing dactyls" when, a half-century later, a mir-
ror-image lower-digestive transaction took place at Saint Elizabeth's Insane Asylum between those two unconscious sex magicians. (See line 782 and accompanying commentary.) They
conjured, not Choronzon, but Bare-Naked Dinkus Boy.

The "Sweet Wizard's" usual predilection for the receptive role
in rectal congress (see note 13) was reversed for the purpose of
buttonholing Choronzon. Conversely, in 1958, in our nation's
capital, the apprentice pitched while the master caught.

208. *And just as he who, with exhausted breath,
      having escaped from the sea to shore,
      turns to the perilous waters and gazes.*

      *So did my soul, that still was fleeing onward,
      Turn itself back to re-behold the pass
      Which never yet a living person left.*
      —*Inferno,* Canto I, 22-27

True to the pattern set in our first canto, our poet ends his book
for *re-readers* with a backward look.

209. *Patience, forbearance, forgiveness: one of the Buddhist practices of
      perfection.*
      —Marc Vincenz

BIBLIOGRAPHY

Adams, J. N. *The Latin Sexual Vocabulary.* Johns Hopkins University
 Press, 1990.

Agrippa, Heinrich Cornelius. *Three Books of Occult Philosophy.* Llewellyn
 Publications, 1992.

Alchemical Texts: Unpublished Manuscripts from the Bodleian Library.
 Oxford: Bodleian Library, 1988.

Alexander, Bishop of Lycopolis. *Of the Manichæans.* Trans. James B. H.
 Hawkins. Ante-Nicene Christian Library, 1869.

Alighieri, Dante. *Inferno.* New York: Doubleday, 2000.

Anonymous. *The Nibelungenlied.* Trans. A. T. Hatto. Penguin Classics,
 1965.

Aristophanes. *The Complete Plays of Aristophanes.* New York: Bantam,
 1962.

Arnold, Matthew. *New Poems.* Ticknor & Fields, 1867.

Ashmole, Elias. *The Alchemical Vision of Sir George Ripley. A facsimile.* Kessinger Publishing LLC, 2010.

Ashmole, Elias. *Elias Ashmole (1617-1692): His Autobiographical and Historical Notes, His Correspondence, and Other Contemporary Sources Relating to His Life and Work, Vol. 4: Texts,* 1673-1701. Ed. C.H. Josten. Oxford: At The Clarendon Press.

Astbury, William. *Textile fibres under the X-rays.* Imperial Chemical Industries limited, 1943.

Athanasius of Alexandria. *On the Incarnation.* Hard Press, 2012.

Auden, W. H. "Under Which Lyre: a Reactionary Tract for the Times." *Phi Beta Kappa Poem,* Harvard, 1946.

Barlas, Evelyn (pseud. Evelyn Douglas). *Love Sonnets.* Cornell UP, 2009.

Barry, Jeff, and Elie Greenwich. "Do Wah Diddy Diddy." Performed by Manfred Mann. Ascot AS 2157 (US). 1964.

Baudelaire, Charles. *The Flowers of Evil.* [New York]: New Directions, 1963.

Beckett, Samuel. *No's Knife.* Calder Publications Ltd., 1967.

Bierce, Ambrose. *The Cynic's Word Book.* London: Arthur F. Bird, 1911.

Blavatsky, Helena P. *The Secret Doctrine: The Synthesis of Science, Religion, and Philosophy.* Pasadena, CA: Theosophical University Press, 1977.

Blavatsky, Helena P. and Michael Gomes. *The Secret Doctrine Commentaries: The Unpublished 1889 Instructions.* The Theosophical Society, 1995.

Blavatsky, Helena P. "The Astral Light." *Transactions of the Blavatsky Lodge*, 1889.

Blavatsky, Helena P. *Isis Unveiled.* Pasadena, CA: Theosophical University Press, 1972.

Blavatsky, Helena P., Ed. *Lucifer: A Theosophical Magazine.* Kessinger Publishing, 2004.

Blavatsky, Helena P. "The New Cycle." *La Revue Théosophique* (1889).

Blavatsky, Helena P., Trans. *Voice of the Silence.* Theosophical University Press, 1992.

Bloom, Harold. *The Anxiety of Influence: A Theory of Poetry.* Oxford University Press US, 1997.

Book of Tobit (Jewish Aprocryphal Literature Series). Trans. Frank Zimmermann. Eisenbrauns, 1958.

Boyle, Robert. *Some Motives and Incentives to the Love of God, Pathetically Discoursed of in a Letter to a Friend.* By the Hon. Robert Boyle. Gale Ecco, 2010.

Bradley, Tom. *Elmer Crowley: a katabasic nekyia.* Oxford, U.K.: Mandrake of Oxford, 2013.

Bradley, Tom. *Fission among the Fanatics.* New York City: Spuyten Duyvil, 2007.

Bradley, Tom. *Hemorrhaging Slave of an Obese Eunuch.* Manchester, U.K.: Dog Horn, 2010.

Bradley, Tom. *Put It Down in a Book.* Drill Press, 2011.

Bradley, Tom. *We'll See Who Seduces Whom: a graphic ekphrasis in verse.* Lafayette, LA: Unlikely Books, 2013.

Bruno, Giordano. *The Heroic Frenzies;.* Chapel Hill: University of North Carolina, 1964.

Byron, George Gordon. *The Bride of Abydos.* Philadelphia: Moses Thomas, 1816.

Carlyle, Thomas. *The French Revolution: A History.* Modern Library, 2002.

Carter, John. *Sex and Rockets: The Occult World of Jack Parsons.* Venice, CA: Feral House, 1999.

Catechism of the Catholic Church. Libreria Editrice Vaticana. United States Conference of Catholic Bishops, 2011.

Chadwick, John, and John Tyrell Killen, Jean Pierre Olivier. *The Knossos Tablets.* Cambridge University Press, 1971.

Charles, R. H., and Hugo Odeberg. *Book of Enoch. 1 Enoch, 2 Enoch (Book of the Secrets of Enoch, 3 Enoch (The Hebrew Book of Enoch), the Measure of the Body (shiur Qoma).* [Los Angeles]: [Work of the Chariot], 1970.

Coleridge, Samuel Taylor. *The Ancient Mariner, Kubla Khan, Christabel.* New York: Macmillan, 1929.

Colonna, Francesco. *Hypnerotomachia Poliphili.* London: Methuen, 1904.

Conway, William Martin. *Literary Remains of Albrecht Dürer,* Cambridge: University, 1889.

Cotten, Trystan Theosophus. *Hung Jury: Testimonies of Genital Surgery by Transsexual Men.* Transgress Press, 2012.

Crick, Francis. *The Astonishing Hypothesis: The Scientific Search For The Soul.* Scribner, 1995.

Crowley, Aleister. *The Confessions of Aleister Crowley: An Autohagiography.* [London]: Arkana, 1989.

Crowley, Aleister. *The Holy Books of Thelema.* York Beach, Me.: S. Weiser, 1983.

Crowley, Aleister. *Moonchild.* Samuel Weiser, 1970.

Cyliani. *Hermes Unveiled.* Edmonds, WA: Alchemical, 1997.

Dallek, Robert. Lyndon B. Johnson: *Portrait of a President.* Oxford University Press USA, 2005.

Dee, John. *De Heptarchia Mystica (Diuinis, Ipsius Creationis, Stabilis Legibus).* British Library under the Catalog Number Sloane 3191.

Dee, John. *The Enochian Invocation of Dr. John Dee.* Heptangle Books, 1983.

Dee, John, and Meric Casaubon. *A True & Faithful Relation of what passed for many Yeers between Dr. John Dee and some Spirits.* Golden Hoard Press, 2011.

De Franciscis, Vittorio. (Editor.) *Signaling Molecules as Targets in Cancer Therapy.* Nova Science Publishers, 2008.

Dio, Cassius, *Roman History, Volume II: Books 12-35.* Loeb Classical Library, 1914.

Dobbs, B. J. T. *Foundations of Newton's Alchemy.* Cambridge UP, 1984.

Donne, John. *Complete Poetry and Selected Prose;.* New York: Modern Library, 1952.

Egyptian Book of the Dead. Trs. Budge, Wallace. Penguin Classics, 2008.

Einstein, Albert. *Letter to the family of Michele Besso,* (March 1955) quoted in *Einstein's God* (NPR). Radio Broadcast.

Eliot, T. S. *Four Quartets.* New York: Harcourt, Brace and, 1943.

Eliot, T. S. *The Frontiers of Criticism: A Lecture.* Minneapolis: University of Minnesota, 1956.

Eliot, T. S., and Christopher Ricks. *Inventions of the March Hare: Poems, 1909-1917.* New York: Harcourt Brace, 1996.

Eliot, T. S. *The Letters of T. S, Eliot, Volume One.* Faber & Faber, 2009.

Eliot, T. S. *The Waste Land: And Other Poems.* London: Faber and Faber, 1971.

Emsley, John. *The Shocking History of Phosphorus.* Pan, 2000.

Elmsley, John. *The 13th Element.* Wiley: New York, 2000.

Emerson, Ralph Waldo. *Collected Works of Ralph Waldo Emerson, Vol. IX. Poems: A Variorum Edition.* Eds. Albert J. von Frank and Thomas Wortham. Harvard University Press, 2011.

Ennius, Quintus. *The tragedies of Ennius.* Cambridge: Cambridge University Press, 1967.

Ephrem of Syria. *A Select Library of the Nicene and Post-Nicene Fathers of the Christian Church,* Volume XIII. Wm. B. Eerdmans Publishing, 1899.

Ernetti, Father Marcello Pellegrino, O.S.B. "Should the *A* go lower still?" *Executive Intelligence Review.* Ed. Lyndon H. LaRouche, Jr. Volume 16, Number 33, August 18, 1989.

Fermi, Enrico. *Elementary Particles.* Yale University Press, 1951.

Flores y Flores, Guillermo, Fr. Bernard Nunes, O.C.D., Edward A. O'Keefe, M.D., and Fr. Robert Skurla *Biography of Veronica Lueken (a.k.a., Veronica of the Cross).* These Last Days Ministries, 2011.

Fox, Margalit. *The Riddle of the Labyrinth: The Quest to Crack and Ancient Code.* Ecco, 2013.

Franz, Marie-Louise von. *Number and Time: Reflections Leading Towards a Unification of Psychology and Physics.* Northwestern University Press, 1974.

Frazer, James George. *The Golden Bough; a Study in Magic and Religion.* New York: Macmillan, 1951.

Freud, Sigmund. *Three Essays on the Theory of Sexuality.* Trans. James Strachey. New York: Basic, 1975.

Gibbon, Edward. *The Decline and Fall of the Roman Empire.* New York: Modern Library, 1932.

Ginsberg, Allen. *Howl and Other Poems.* San Francisco: City Lights Pocket Poets, No. 4, 1956.

Goethe, Johann Wolfgang von. *Italian Journey.* Trans. W. H. Auden and Elizabeth Mayer. Penguin Classics, 1992.

Goldman, Harry L. "Nikola Tesla's Bold Adventure." *American West* (1971).

Goodwin, Edward J. "Gerardus Craesius' Homerus Hebraus Sive Historia: Hebraorum Ab Homero." *Miscellaneous Notes and Queries* 12 (1894).

Green, Paul. *Jennifer Jones: The Life and Films*. McFarland, 2011.

Grundy, Stephan, trans. *Gilgamesh*. New York: William Morrow, 2000.

Guiterrez, Diego. *The Americas (maps)*, 1562. British Library.

Haberman, A. M., and Joseph Haker. *The Alphabet of Ben Sira*. London: Valmadonna Trust Library, 1997.

Haeffner, Mark. *The Dictionary of Alchemy: From Maria Prophetissa to Isaac Newton*. Thorsons Publications,1995.

Hall, Manly P. *The Secret Teachings of All Ages: An Encyclopedic Outline of Masonic, Hermetic, Qabbalistic, and Rosicrucian Symbolical Philosophy : Being an Interpretation of the Secret Teachings Concealed within the Rituals, Allegories, and Mysteries of the Ages*. New York: Jeremy P. Tarcher/Penguin, 2003.

Hammer, M. F., and Redd, A. J., Wood E. T., M. R. Bonner, H. Jarjanazi, T. Karafet, S. Santachiara-Benerecetti, A. Oppenheim, M. A. Jobling, T. Jenkins, H. Ostrer, and B. Bonné-Tamir. "Jewish and Middle Eastern non-Jewish populations share a common pool of Y-chromosome biallelic haplotypes." *Proceedings of the National Academy of Sciences of the United States of America*, 97, June 2000.

Harriot, Thomas. *A Briefe and True Report of the New Found Land of Virginia. A facsimile of the 1588 edition.* Book Jungle, 2007.

Herodotus. *Histories.* Trans. A.D. Godley. Cambridge: Harvard University Press, 1920.

Sir Hillary, Edmund. *No Latitude for Error.* Hodder & Stoughton, 1961.

Holmyard, E.J. *The Book of Knowledge Acquired Concerning the Cultivation of Gold.* Paul Geuthner, 1923.

Homer. *The Iliad.* Trans. John Murray. London: Walton and Maberly, 1862.

Horace. *Odes and Epodes.* Loeb, 2004.

Horton, Alice. (Translator). *The Lay of the Nibelungs: Metrically Translated from the Old German Text.* G. Bell and Sons, London, 1898.

Huxley, Aldous. *Antic Hay.* New York: Doran, 1923.

Huxley, Aldous. *The Devils of Loudun.* New York: Harper, 1952.

Huxley, Aldous. *Eyeless in Gaza.* New York And: Harper & Bros., 1936.

Iamblichus. *On the Mysteries of the Egyptians, Chaldeans, and Assyrians.* Bertram Dobell, 1895.

I Likes Babies and Infinks. Dirs. Fleischer, Dave and Seymour Kneitel. Fleischer Studios, 1937. Film.

James, M. R., Trans. *Acts of Peter, in The Apocryphal New Testament.* Clarendon, 1924.

Jonson, Ben. *The Devil Is an Ass.* Manchester, England: New York, 1994.

Jonson, Ben. *Discoveries: Made upon Men and Matter: And Some Poems.* London: Cassell, 1889.

Joyce, James. *Finnegans Wake.* New York: Viking, 1939.

Joyce, James. *A Portrait of the Artist as a Young Man.* Dover, 1994.

Joyce, James. *Ulysses.* A Facsimile of the First Edition Published in Paris in 1922. Orchises Press, 1998.

Jung, C. G. *The Collected Works.* Eds. Read, Herbert, Michael Fordham, and Gerhard Adler. New York: Pantheon, 1953.

Jung, C. G., *The Red Book.* Trs. Shamdasani, Sonu and Mary Kyburz, John Peck. The Philemon Foundation and W.W. Norton & Co., 2009.

Justin Martyr, and Athenagoras. *The Complete Works of Justin Martyr and Athenagoras.* Trans. George Reith. Pneuma, 2013.

Juvenal. *The Satires.* Trans. Niall Rudd. Oxford University Press, USA, 2008.

Klijn, Albertus Frederik Johannes. *The Acts of Thomas: Introduction, Text, and Commentary* (Supplements to Novum Testamentum, Book 108). Brill, 2003.

Kafka, Franz. *The Complete Short Stories of Franz Kafka.* London: Vintage, 1999.

Kelley, Edward, and John Dee. *The Complete Enochian Dictionary: A Dictionary of the Angelic Language As Revealed to Dr. John Dee and Edward Kelley.* Weiser Books, 2001.

Kendall, Roy. Christopher Marlowe and Richard Baines: *Journeys Through the Elizabethan Underground.* Farleigh Dickinson University Press, 2004.

King James Bible. Nashville, TN: Holman Bible, 1973.

Krassner, Paul. "The Parts That Were Left Out of the Kennedy Book." *The Realist* 74 (1967).

Krassa, Peter. *Father Ernetti's Chronovisor: The Creation and Disappearance of the World's First Time Machine.* Boca Raton, Florida: New Paradigm Books, 2000.

Krill, Aaron J., Lane S. Palmer, and Jeffrey S. Palmer. "Complications of Circumcision." *Scientific World Journal,* 2011.

Lambert, W. G., and A. R. Millard. *Atra-Hasis: The Babylonian Story of the Flood with The Sumerian Flood Story.* Oxford at Clarendon Press, 1970.

Laertius, Diogenes. *Lives of Eminent Philosophers.* London: Wm. Hinemann, 1925.

Larrington, Carolyne, Trans. *The Poetic Edda*. Oxford UP, 2009.

LaVey, Anton. *The Satanic Bible*. London: Paperback Division of W.H. Allen &, 1977.

Levin, Ira. *Rosemary's Baby; a Novel*. New York: Random House, 1967.

Loy, Mina. *Virgins Plus Curtains*. Press of the Good Mountain, 1981

Lucan. *Pharsalia*. Cornell University Press, 1993.

Magnus of Sens, *Libellus de mysterio baptismatis*. (Private collection.)

Maier, Michael. *A Subtle Allegory Concerning the Secrets of Alchemy: Very Useful to Possess and Pleasant to Read*. Edmonds, Wa.: Alchemical, 1984.

Malthus, Thomas. *An Essay on the Principle of Population*. Empire Books, 2013.

Marlowe, Christopher. *Four Plays: Tamburlaine, Parts One and Two, The Jew of Malta, Edward II and Dr Faustus*. Bloomsbury Methuen Drama, 2011.

Marlowe, Christopher, and George Chapman. *Hero and Leander: 1598*. London: Etchells and Macdonald, 1924.

Martial. *Epigrams*. Trans. D. R. Shackleton Bailey. Loeb, 1993.

Maternus, Firmicus. *The Error of the Pagan Religions*. New York: Newman, 1970.

Mathers, S. L. MacGregor, Aleister Crowley, and Hymenaeus Beta. *The Goetia: The Lesser Key of Solomon the King: Lemegeton--Clavicula Salomonis Regis.* York Beach, Me.: Samuel Weiser, 1995.

McKenna, Terence. *Third Lecture on Alchemy.* Wetlands Preserve, 1998. Audio.

Mede, Joseph. *Clavis Apocalyptica (On the Sun of the Bestial Heaven).* London: J. G. & F. Rivington, 1833.

Melville, Herman. *Moby Dick.* New York: Farrar, Straus, and Giroux, 1997.

Meyer, Marvin W. and Robinson, James M. (Translators). *The Nag Hammadi Scriptures: The Revised and Updated Translation of Sacred Gnostic Texts.* HarperOne, 2009.

Midal, Fabrice. *Chögyam Trungpa: His Life and Vision.* Boston: Shambhala, 2004.

Milton, John. *Paradise Lost.* New York: Odyssey, 1935.

Milton, John. *Samson Agonistes.* London: Oxford University Press, 1957.

Morris, Jan. *Conundrum: An Extraordinary Personal Narrative of Transsexualism.* Harcourt Brace Jovanovich, 1974.

Nabokov, Vladimir Vladimirovich. "On Discovering a Butterfly" *New Yorker* (1943).

Nabokov, Vladimir Vladimirovich. *Lectures on Literature.* New York: Harcourt Brace Jovanovich, 1980.

Nabokov, Vladimir Vladimirovich. *Novels, 1955-1962: Lolita, Pnin, Pale Fire, Lolita a Screenplay.* New York, NY: Literary Classics of the United States, 1996.

Nabokov, Vladimir Vladimirovich. *Pale Fire: A Novel.* New York: Putnam, 1962.

Neuburg, Victor Benjamin. *The Triumph of Pan.* London: Equinox, 1910.

Neuser, Jacob. *Mishnah: A New Translation.* Yale University Press, 1991.

Newton, Isaac. *Sr George Ripley lived in ye days of Edward ye 4th to whome he wrote a Epistle.* Cambridge, Keynes MS. 51, King's College Library, Cambridge University.

Newton, Isaac. *Hermetis Tabula Smaragdina.* Keynes MS. 13, King's College Library, Cambridge University.

Nietzsche, Friedrich Wilhelm. *On the Genealogy of Morals.* New York: Vintage, 1967.

Northern Nevada Writing Project Teacher-Researcher Group. *Team Teaching.* Stenhouse, 1996.

Norton, Thomas. *The Ordinall of Alchemy.* Kessinger Publishing, 2010.

Nostradamus. *The Complete Prophecies of Nostradamus.* Oyster Bay, NY: Nostradamus, 1969.

O'Neil, Moira Eileen. *The cultural construction of war and mental trouble: World War I veterans, masculinity and psychiatry at St. Elizabeth's Hospital.* ProQuest, UMI Dissertation Publishing, 2011.

Orwell, George. *1984: A Novel.* New York, NY: Published by Signet Classic, 1977.

Ovid. *The Metamorphoses of Ovid.* New York: Harcourt Brace, 1993.

Paracelsus. (Hohenheim, Philippus Theophrastus Aureolus Bombastus von) *Paracelsus: Selected Writings.* Trans. Jolande Jacobi. Princeton, NJ: Princeton UP, 1979.

Parry, Milman. *The Making of Homeric Verse: The Collected Papers of Milman Parry.* Oxford University Press, USA, 1987.

Parsons, Jack. *The Collected Writings: The Book of Babalon, The Book of Antichrist, and Other Writings.* Ed. Hymnenaeus Beta. Teitan Press, 2008.

Parsons, Jack. *Three Essays on Freedom.* Teitan Press, 2008.

Pauley, Jane. *Skywriting: A Life Out of the Blue.* Random House, 2004.

Pauling, Linus. "Discovery of the Elements (Weeks, Mary Elvira)." *Journal of Chemical Education* 34.1 (1957): 51.

Pentateuch and Haftorahs: Hebrew Text English Translation and Commentary. Ed. Hertz, J.H. The Soncino Press, 1960.

Philo Judaeus: works. Trans. F. H. Colson and G. H. Whitaker. Cambridge, MA: Harvard University Press, 1929.

Pifer, Ellen. *Vladimir Nabokov's Lolita: A Casebook.* Oxford: Oxford UP, 2003.

Plato. *Cratylus.* Hackett Publications, 1998.

Pliny the Elder. *Natural History.* Trans. Trevor Murphy. Oxford: Oxford University Press, 2004.

Plutarch, *Fall of the Roman Republic.* Ed. Robin Seager. Trans. Rex Warner. Penguin Classics; Revised edition, 2006.

Poe, Edgar Allan. *Collected Works.* Canterbury Classics, 2011.

Polo, Marco. *The Travels of Marco Polo.* Signet Classics, 2004.

Poole, Rebecca. "Biomimetics: In Pursuit of Natural Sources of Inspiration." *The Society for Experimental Biology Bulletin,* January 2007.

Pope Gregory I. *The Dialogues of Saint Gregory: Surnamed the Great; Pope of Rome & the First of That Name. Divided Into Four Books, Wherein He Entreateth of the Lives and Miracles of the Saints of Italy and of the Eternity of Men's Souls.* Cornell University Library, 2009.

Posidonious, *The Translation of the Fragments. Cambridge Classical Tests and Commentaries.* Cambridge University Press; 2nd edition, 2003.

Pound, Ezra. *Cantos*. London: Faber & Faber, 1954.

Pound, Ezra. "In a Station of the Metro." *Poetry* (1913).

Pound, Ezra. "Marianne Moore and Mina Loy," review of *Others* 1917, *Little Review*, March 1918; rpt. in *Ezra Pound, Selected Prose 1909-1965*. New York: New Directions, 1973.

Pound, Ezra. *The Selected Letters 1907-1941*. New Directions, 1971.

Proust, Marcel. *Remembrance of Things Past*. Trans. C. K. Scott-Moncrieff. New York: Random House, 1934.

Pseudo-Dionysius. *Complete Works*. Paulist Press, 1988.

Puleo, Stephen. *Dark Tide: The Great Boston Molasses Flood of 1919*. Beacon Press, 2003.

Raleigh, Sir Walter. *Selected Writings*. Penguin Classics, 1986.

Regardie, Israel. *The Tree of Life: A Study in Magic*. Weiser, 1972.

Ricci, Matteo. *China in the Sixteenth Century*. Random House, 1953.

"Richard Baines to the Privy Council." *Norton Anthology of English Literature*. W. W. Norton, 2012.

Ripley, George. *The Compound of Alchymy; Or, the Twelve Gates Leading to the Discovery of the Philosopher's Stone (Liber Duodecim Portarum) 1591*. Ed. Stanton J. Linden. Ashgate, 2001.

Ripley, George. *Cantilena Riplaei*. (Private collection.)

Rosencreutz, Christian. *The Hermetick Romance, Or, The Chymical Wedding.* Trans. E. Foxcroft. London: Printed by A. Sowle, 1690.

Rosemary's Baby. Dir. Polanski, Roman. Paramount Pictures, 1968. Film.

Segar, E. C. *Alice the Goon.* Thimble Theater comic strip, 1933-7, King Features Syndicate.

Sepher Derekh Hayyim Hash-Shalem: Massekheth Abhoth 'im Perush Rashi ... Ve-gham ... Be'ur ... Derekh Hayyim. J. Lehmann, 1961.

Seymour-Jones, Carole. *Painted Shadow: A Life of Vivienne Eliot.* Nan A. Talese, 2002.

Shackleton, Sir Ernest. *South: A Memoir of the Endurance Voyage.* London: Robinson, 1998.

Shakespeare, William. *Complete Works.* London: Oxford University Press, 1974.

Shaw, Bernard, and Arnold Moss. *Back to Methuselah.* New York: Samuel French, 1957.

Shelley, Mary Wollstonecraft. *Frankenstein; or The Modern Prometheus.* London: Oxford U.P., 1969.

Shipman, Pat. *Femme Fatale: Love, Lies, and the Unknown Life of Mata Hari.* New York: W. Morrow, 2007.

Shreck, Nikolas, and Zeena Shreck. *Demons of the Flesh.* Creation Books, 2002.

Simms, Joseph. *Physiognomy Illustrated, or Nature's Revelations of Character: A Description of the Mental, Moral and Volitive Dispositions of Mankind, as Manifested in the Human Form and Countenance.* D.M. Bennett, 1887.

Simpson, Louis. *Modern Poets of France: A Bilingual Anthology.* Story Line Press, 1997.

Snow White and the Seven Dwarfs. Dir. Hand, David et. al. Walt Disney, 1937. Film

Song of Bernadette. Dir. King, Henry. Twentieth Century-Fox, 1943. Film.

Sophocles. *Oedipus The King, Oedipus at Colonus, Antigone.* Trans, David Grene. University of Chicago Press, 1991.

Śrī Kālī Pūjā: Kali Puja. Trans. Saraswati, Swami Satyananda. 1st World Publishing, 1999.

Stein, Gertrude. *Selected Writings of Gertrude Stein.* Vintage, 1990.

Stoney, George Johnstone. *The Electron Theory: A Popular Introduction to the New Theory of Electricty and Magnetism.* London ; New York : Longmans, Green and Co., 1916.

Strachey, William. *A Dictionary of Powhatan.* Evolution, 2005.

Strachey, William, and Silvester Jourdain. *A Voyage to Virginia in 1609: Two Narratives: Strachey's "True Reportory" and Jourdain's Discovery of the Bermudas.* University of Virginia Press, 2013.

Sturluson, Snorri. *Prose Edda.* Trans. Jesse L. Byock. Penguin Classics, 2006.

Suetonius. *Lives of the Twelve Caesars.* Oxford University Press, 2009.

Swift, Jonathan. *The Complete Works of Jonathan Swift ...Containing Interesting and Valuable Papers Not Hitherto Published, and an Autograph Letter.* London: Bell and Daldy, 1869.

Tacitus, *The Annals.* Trans. Cynthia Damn. Penguin Classics, 2013.

Tesla, Nikola. *Colorado Springs Notes.* Important Books, 2013.

Tesla, Nikola. *The Problem of Increasing Human Energy.* Kessinger Publishing, 2010.

Theatrum Chemicum Britannicum, Ed. Elias Ashmole (1617-1692). London: Printed by J. Grismond for Nath: Brooke, at the angel in Cornhill, 1692. Medical Heritage Library.

Thoreau, Henry David. *A Week on the Concord and Merrimack Rivers.* Princeton, NJ: Princeton University Press, 1980.

Tolliot, Siegfried. *Bare-Naked Dinkus Boy Meets Jane Pauley.* Unpublished Manuscript.

Tolliot, Siegfried. "The Root of Pound's Wet Black Bough." *Kanorado Review of the Collective Humanities* 3 (1981).

Tolliot, Siegfried. *Incantations of a Mad Man.* Padua: Edizioni Ermetica, 1969 (limited edition).

Tolliot, Siegfried. *The Private Letters and Email Messages of a Priapic Eunuch, 1958-2012.* Unpublished Manuscript.

Valborg, Helen. "The City." *Hermes Magazine* (1981).

Vincenz, Marc. *Gods of a Ransacked Century.* Unlikely Books, 2013.

Vincenz, Marc. *Mao's Mole: A History in Rhetoric and Verse.* NeoPoiesis Press, 2013.

Vincenz, Marc. *The Propaganda Factory: or Speaking of Trees.* New York City: Spuyten Duyvil, 2013.

Vincenz, Marc. *Pull of the Gravitons.* Right Hand Pointing, 2012.

Voltaire. *La Pucelle, the Maid of Orleans: An Heroic-comical Poem in Twenty-one Cantos.* London: Lutetian Society, 1899.

Wagner, Richard. *The Ring of the Nibelung.* Trans. Andrew Porter. W. W Norton, 1977.

Welling, Georg von. *Opus Mago-cabbalisticum Et Theosophicum: In Which The Origin, Nature, Characteristics, And Use Of Salt , Sulfur and Mercury are Described in Three Parts Together with much Wonderful Mathematical, Theosophical, Magical, and Mystical Material as Well as Thoughts on the Creation of Metals and Minerals in Nature, Many Curious Mago-Cabbalistic*

Illustrations, and a Key to the Entire Work. Also Included Are Essays on Divine Wisdom and an Appendix of Several Quite Rare and Precious Alchemical Pieces. Trans. Joseph G. McVeigh. Weiser Books, 2006.

Whistler, James McNeill. *The Gentle Art of Making Enemies.* New York: F. Stokes & Brother, 1890.

"White Phosphorus." *Jerusalem Media and Communication Centre,* 2009.

Whitman, Walt. *Memories of President Lincoln.* New York: Little Leather Library Corporation, 1916.

An Appalachian Symposium: Essays Written in Honor of Cratis D. Williams. Ed. J. W. Williamson. Boone State University Press, 1977.

Wise, Michael O., and Martin G. Jr. Abegg and Edward M. Cook. *The Dead Sea Scrolls: A New Translation.* HarperSanFrancisco, 2005.

Wolter, Xavier F. M. G. *Notes in Antique Folklore on the basis of Pliny's Natural History.* Amsterdam, 1935.

Xin, Xu. *Legends of the Chinese Jews of Kaifeng.* Ktav Publications, 1995.

Yeats, W.B. *The Collected Works of W.B. Yeats.* Ed. Richard J. Finneran. Scribner, 1997.

Zeno of Elea. *Text With Translation and Notes.* Trans. Lee, H. D. P. Adolf M. Hakkert, 1967.

Zosimos of Panopolis. *Corpus Alchemicum Arabicum.* Daimon Verlag, 2007.

Index

B

hypertrophy of septum and nares (as a physiognomic indicator of Levantine ethnicity) 74

Hypnerotomachia Poliphili 57, 104, 193

I

L

M

Marc Vincenz

Born in Hong Kong during the height of the Cultural Revolution, Marc Vincenz has spent most of his life on the road. He has lived in England, Switzerland, Spain, Hong Kong, China, the United States, and has traveled far and wide to such remote locations such as central Siberia, the Amazon Rainforest, Tibet, India's Thar Desert, and China's Kun Lun Mountains. After many years of business and travel in the Far East, he finally settled in Shanghai in the 90s.

His work has appeared in many journals both online and in print, including *Washington Square Review, Fourteen Hills, The Canary, The Bitter Oleander, Superstition Review, Crab Creek Review, The Battersea Review, St. Petersburg Review, Tears in the Fence, Pirene's Fountain, Exquisite Corpse, The Potomac, Poetry Salzburg Review, Spillway, Stirring, MiPOesias* and *Guernica*. His work has been translated into German, Russian and Romanian. He has been awarded several grants from the Swiss Arts Council for his translations.

His recent books include *The Propaganda Factory, or Speaking of Trees* (2011); *Gods of a Ransacked Century* (Unlikely Books, 2013), *Mao's Mole* (Neopoiesis Press, 2013), *Beautiful Rush* (Unlikely Books, 2014) and a meta-novel, *Behind the Wall at the Sugar Works* (Spuyten Duyvil, 2014). A new English-German bilingual collection, *Additional Breathing Exercises* was recently released by Wolfbach Verlag, Zurich (2014). He is also completing a spoken-word album to be released by Neuroshell Records, New York. He is Publisher and Executive Editor of *MadHat* (*Mad Hatters' Review*) and MadHat Press and Coeditor-in-Chief of *Fulcrum*: an annual of poetry and aesthetics.

He now divides his time between Reykjavik, Zurich, Berlin and New York City.

Tom Bradley

Tom Bradley has published twenty-six volumes of fiction, essays, screenplays and poetry. Various of his novels have been nominated for the Editor's Book Award, the New York University Bobst Prize, and the AWP Series. 3:AM Magazine in Paris gave him their Nonfiction Book of the Year Award in 2007 and 2009.

His journalism and criticism have appeared in such publications as Salon.com, and are featured in Arts & Letters Daily. Denis Dutton, editor of the site ("among the most influential media personalities in the world," according to Time Magazine), wrote as follows:

> *Tom Bradley is one of the most exasperating, offensive, pleasurable, and brilliant writers I know. I recommend his work to anyone with spiritual fortitude and a taste for something so strange that it might well be genius.*

Recent ventures with artists Nick Patterson and David Aronson include *Family Romance* (Jaded Ibis, 2012), *Elmer Crowley: a katabasic nekyia* (Mandrake of Oxford, 2013), and *We'll See Who Seduces Whom: a graphic ekphrasis in verse* (Unlikely Books, 2013).

This Wasted Land and Its Chymical Illuminations is the third collaborative book for which Tom Bradley has furnished footnotes. The previous two are *Epigonesia* (with Kane X. Faucher, BlazeVOX, 2011) and *Felicia's Nose* (with Carol Novack, MadHat, 2012)

Further curiosity can be indulged at tombradly.org.

18590158R00148

Made in the USA
Middletown, DE
13 March 2015